GUTTER PARADISE ADELE RENAULT

FOREWORD: Carlo McCormick
INTRO: Alexandre Latscha

PHOTOGRAPHY:
page 20, 32, 48 Pref
page 30, 31, 64 Mathieu Latscha
page 58, 59, 68 Asato Iida
page 61 left Ben Hughes
page 61, 69 Kenn 김병구
page 63 Cas Lambrechts
page 64, 65 Alexandre Baloup
page 66 Dan Verbruggen – Ausilio Photography
page 70, 71 Camila Álvarez
page 72 Martin Smith
page 73, 76 Marian Medic
page 74 Jean-Christpohe Renault
page 77 Veronique Gillet
page 78 Justin Gardner
page 79 Pac 黃思強
page 81 Ari Sturm
page83 Martha Cooper

distributed in the United States and Canada
by SCB Distributors

ISBN 978-90-828907-1-6
NUR 640

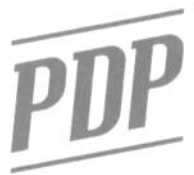

www. pdpgallery.com
www.adelerenault.com

ADELE RENAULT

Gutter Paradise

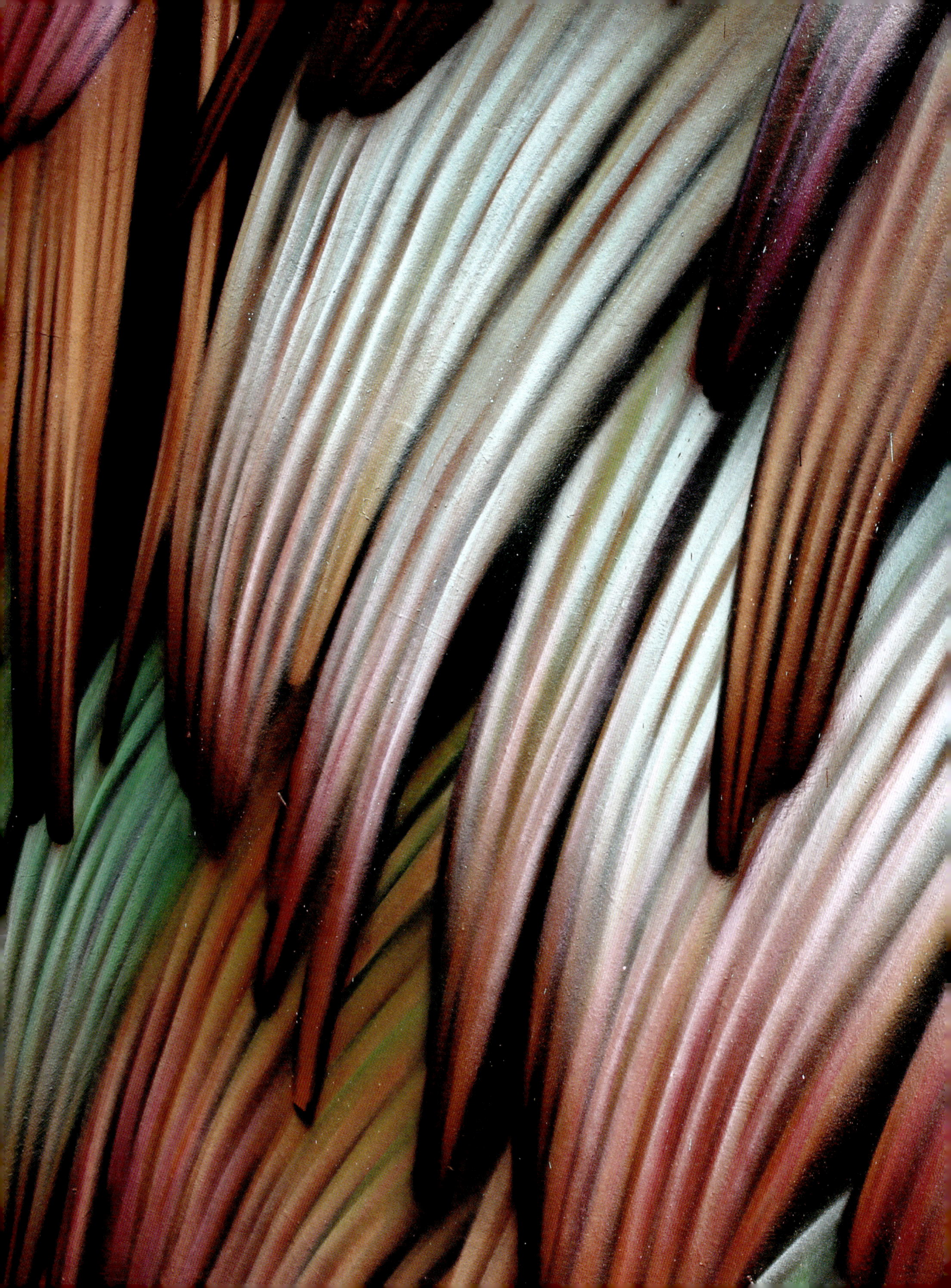

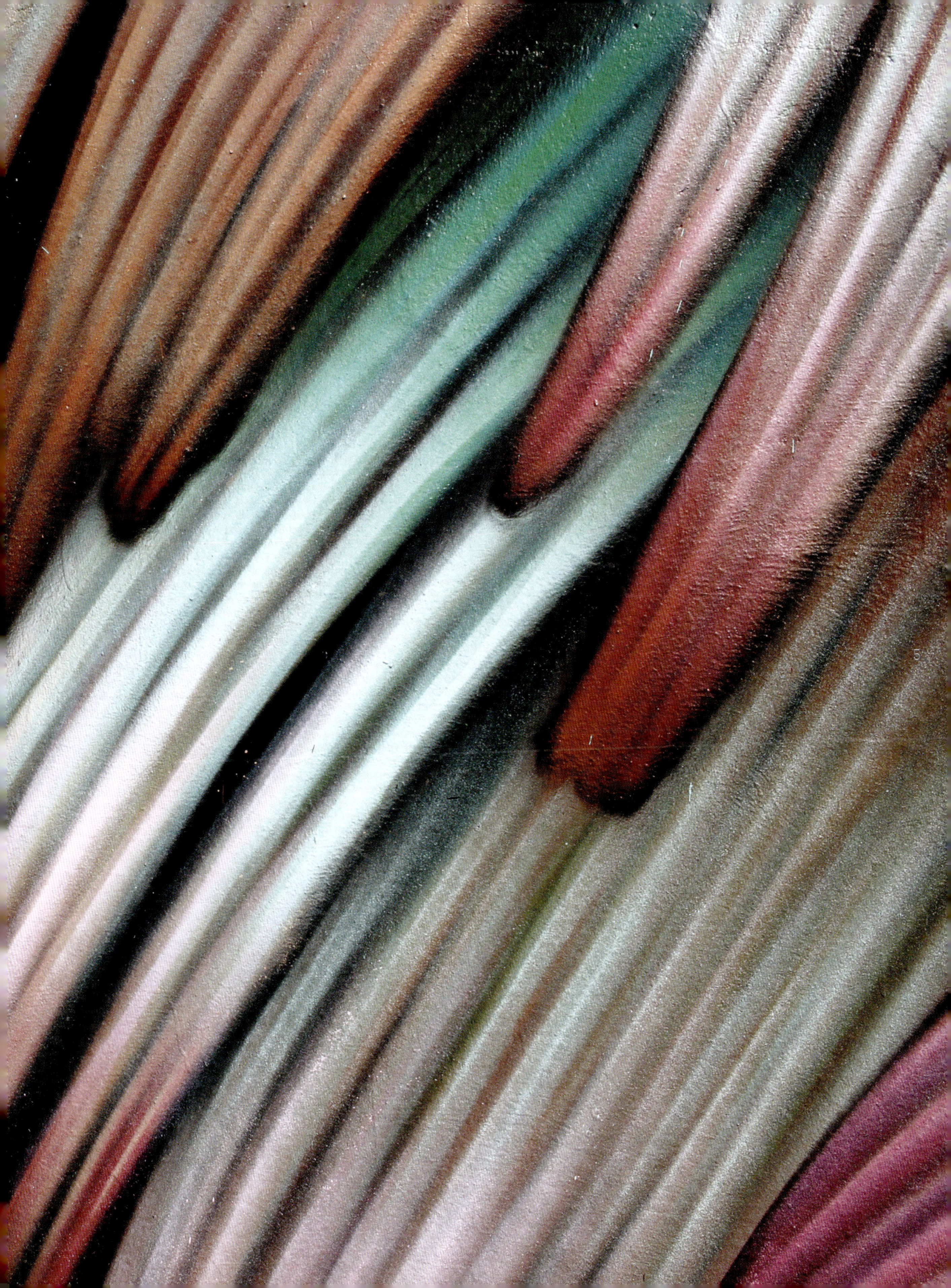

FOREWORD

by Carlo McCormick

ADELE RENAULT: MUSIC TO WATCH BIRDS BY

We are birds of a feather, clay pigeons, night owls, and canaries in the coalmine, odd ducks and ugly ducklings all. Flying south for the winter, spreading our wings or simply learning how to fly, feathering our nests, singing our swan song, learning about the birds and the bees and counting our chickens before they hatch, but just maybe with all that we can yet be free as a bird. We might fly the coop, proud as a peacock, with an eagle eye or at least a bird's eye view, but early birds get the worm and we chicken out, not even eating like a bird. Whether hawks or doves, are we then wise as an owl or just silly geese too bird-brained and pigeon-toed clumsy to know how inept we really are? It's as easy as duck soup knowing that there is a pecking order, and though we might try to kill two birds with one stone we are just as likely to be the lame duck laying an egg, neither first nor last, amidst a murder of crows and a flock of seagulls, looking for the right punch-line to why the chicken crossed the road and pondering such existential questions as which came first the chicken or the egg?

Do any of these American idioms even translate, or are they even particularly American? We have an uncanny way of thinking we invented everything while at the same time expecting that everything about us is universal. Personally I'd like to believe that the language of birds is somehow common to all, or as they say, what's good for the goose is good for the gander. What is certain is that birds occupy a singular place in the human imagination, metaphor for freedom and fancy, yet allegory for our Icarus-like hubris. Of course we all want to fly, on a wing and a prayer, so the capacity for some species to do this as if the simplest of things enthralls us like an impossible dream. They are our closest friends and neighbors, pernicious pests and objects of unspeakable wonder, and for many of us city folk pretty much the only wildlife we know. The grace and glory of Adele Renault's bird paintings is that she manages to mine the familiarity by which we identify with birds while allowing them their marvelous difference as an alien species. Without the cloying tropes of anthropomorphism by which all manner of animals have been imbued with sentimental humanness in cartoons and other kid-friendly fictions, Renault lets us see her birds as like us but not, of our world but crucially unbound from our earthly concerns.

On canvas, on our walls and in our homes, her feathered friends are wildlife and pets feral yet tame; wary companions that sing to us in silent flights of fancy yet perched in waiting, alive and uncontainable, ready for an open window to make their escape. So present and personable, they dovetail perfectly with her human portraiture, proffering a sense that her paintings of people, rendered with the same attention and loving care as her birds, are perhaps too like all of us, curious birds themselves. Outside, on buildings as public art in sync with the wider muralist movement that is reshaping our cities around the world, Adele's sensuously plumed avifauna is not simply just at home but potent embodiments of the home itself. Beyond all their allegorical associations birds remain first and foremost metaphors for the domestic. We build birdhouses and birdbaths, aviaries, chicken coops and hen houses, but these are just more proximately viewable approximations for the hold that their nesting takes within our imagination. Somehow, just as captivating as the wonder of flight, there is a joy and empathy we all take in the image of a bird carefully building its nest, sitting vigil on its eggs, the hatching of a fledging or the tender mercy of a parent feeding their young worms along the way. Even though most of us have neither the passion nor patience of dedicated ornithologists, we are all somehow birdwatchers, or as they are familiarly known- birders. As an artist Adele Renault reminds us of that as the simplest of pleasures, and somehow the most human of our attributes.

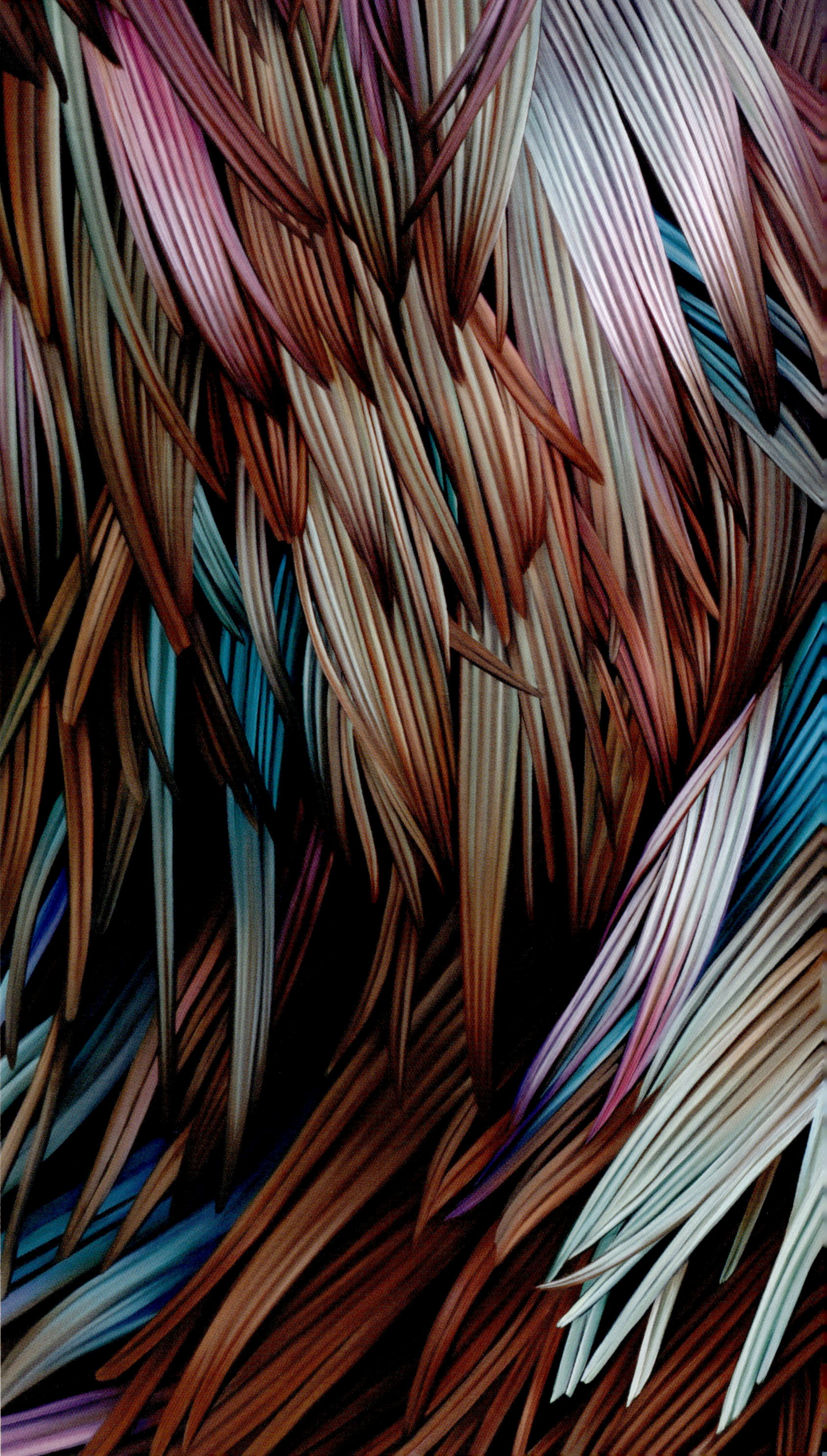

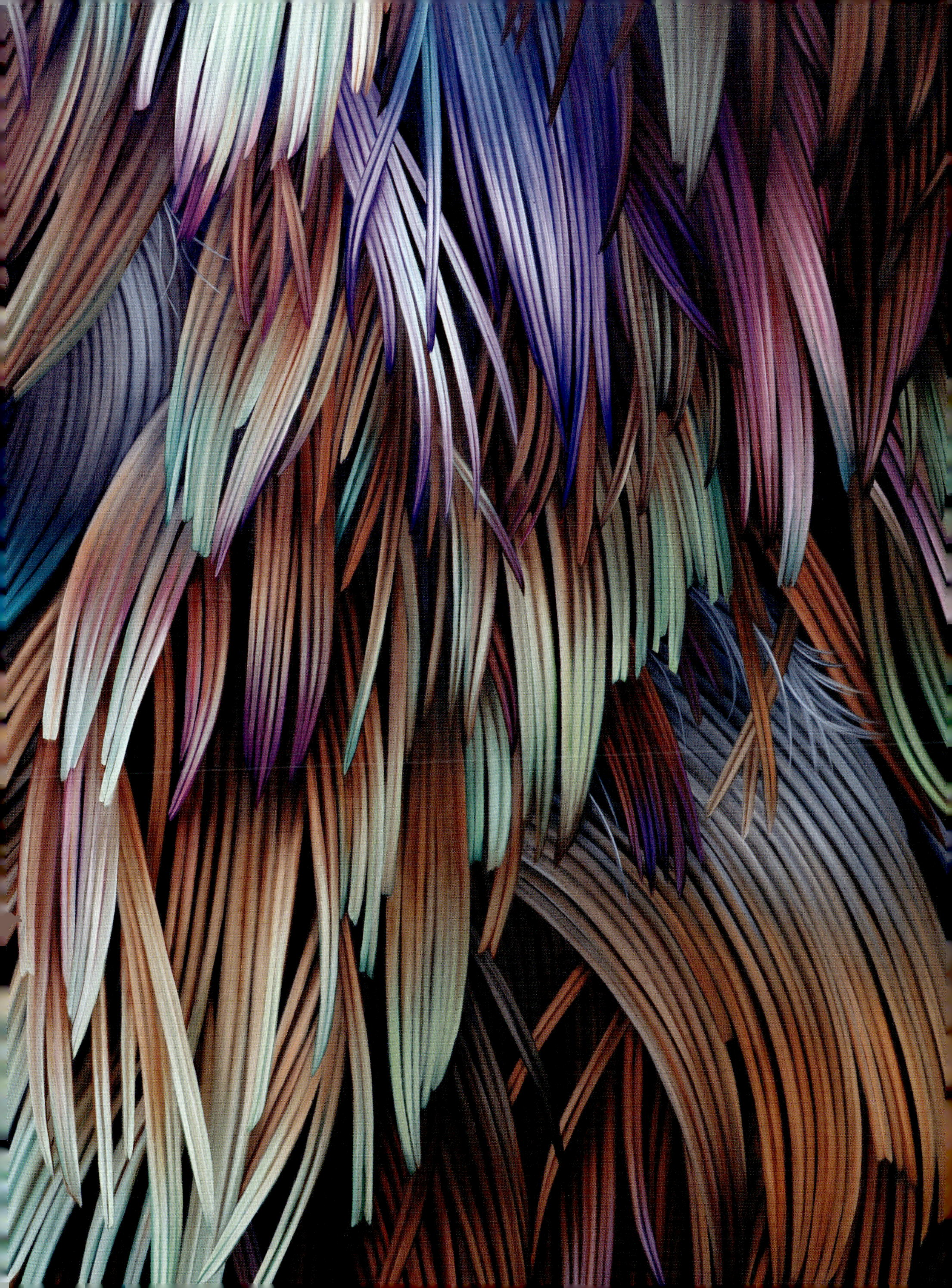

INTRO

by Alexandre Latscha

To follow Adele Renault is to fly away with her paintings, throughout the globe, without borders; Belgium, United States, France, Burkina Faso, Netherlands, Taiwan, Italy, Croatia... The world is a stage for the Belgian artist.

In October 2019, our paths crossed in California. I recall a visit to her studio when she was starting the production of her largest *Gutter Paradise* oil painting: the number 11. Her atelier looked over a mural by Kenny Scharf, in the heart of West Adams, a historic neighborhood in South Los Angeles. A wild area, emblematic of the culture she immerses herself in and where Adele had landed.

The urban art scene is a tight knit world in which Adele has made a name for herself over the years. The force of her commitment to her art, her ability with spray paint and her vast network could lead you to believe that she comes straight out of 80's New York, until we discover she is from Belgium and barely in her thirties.

Mile after mile, fascinated by her parents' travel stories, Adele seems only to be moved by adventure. There is a powerful bond among the Renault family, a particular sensitivity rooted in a family of artists with a collective conviction that allows each one to express themselves and create freely. We find the ebb and flow of it at every moment of her life: freedom essential to constructing her identity. Influences always intersect like in the series of portraits *Men of Integrity* of 2016, her first monochrome desires that we rediscover in the last *Gutter Paradise* paintings of 2020.

Backed by her total technical mastery, what strikes me in Adele's work is her capacity for precision whatever the medium is.

Passionnée et passionnante, suivre Adèle Renault c'est s'envoler avec sa peinture, à travers le monde, sans frontières. Belgique, États-Unis, France, Burkina Faso, Pays Bas, Taiwan, Italie, Croatie...
Pas de limite de décor pour l'artiste belge mais partout l'expression d'une culture libre.

C'est dans son atelier californien, en octobre 2019, que je retrouve Adèle, aux prémices de la production de son plus grand *Gutter Paradise* à l'huile : le numéro 11.
Installée face aux fresques de Kenny Scharf, Adèle Renault fait escale au cœur de West Adams, quartier historique du sud de Los Angeles, populaire et en marge, symbole de la culture dont elle s'imprègne.
Dans le petit milieu de l'art urbain, Adèle Renault a depuis longtemps une grande réputation. Toujours en action, ouverte sur le monde, on l'imagine tout droit venue du New York des années 80 et on la découvre à peine trentenaire. C'est la force de son engagement artistique.

A l'épreuve des kilomètres, fascinée par les récits de voyage de ses parents, Adèle semble n'être intéressée que par l'aventure. Il existe un lien très fort chez les Renault, une sensibilité particulière ; celle d'une famille d'artistes avec une conviction collective qui permet à chacun de s'exprimer et de créer librement. On en retrouve l'onde à tous les moments de sa vie d'artiste; une liberté essentielle à la construction de son identité. Des influences s'entrecroisent constamment comme dans la série de portraits, *Hommes intègres* de 2016; premières envies monochromes que l'on redécouvre dans les dernières toiles de 2020.

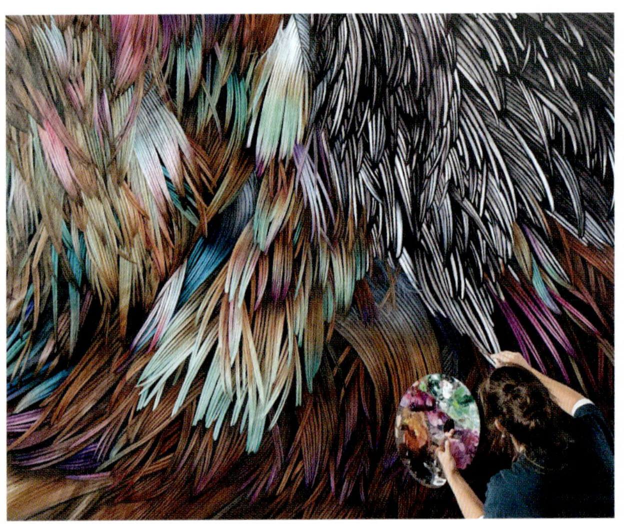

work in progress *Gutter Paradise #11*

As her exploration gains ground, a series of oil paintings appear: *Gutter Paradise*. Adele Renault succeeds in creating a universal and sensitive language. It is no longer a matter of words or gazes but the power of sensation. Gutter Paradise, like her portraits, appeals to our collective memory and our capacity for appropriation. The explosions of colors in these pictorial creations evoke memories that seem almost artificial to us, like a supernatural fauna. *Gutter Paradise* comes from the street and responds to the codes of repetitive paintings.

In front of her, there is just a two-meter canvas. I watched Adèle start making *Gutter Paradise #11* and her desire and determination hit me again. It is the very expression of total painting that we all want to defend. You have to see Adele Renault in action, like so many others, to soak up this vibration. A force that only painting, in all its forms of expression, can provide.

From her first pigeon studies to the meticulous depictions of her feathers, Adele Renault has matured this new series; this paradise staged from nothing: from a detail that has become the subject.

Forte d'une maîtrise technique totale, ce qui frappe chez Adèle est cette capacité de précision quel que soit le médium.

Au fur et à mesure de son exploration, une série de peintures à l'huile, "*Gutter Paradise*" apparaît. Adele réussit à créer un langage universel et sensible. Ce n'est plus alors une histoire de mots ou de regards mais la force d'une sensation. A l'instar de ses portraits, la série en appelle à notre mémoire collective et notre capacité d'appropriation. L'explosion des couleurs dans ces créations picturales nous évoquent des souvenirs qui nous apparaissent presque artificiels, telle une faune surnaturelle. Initié dans la rue, son travail répond aux codes d'une peinture de répétition.

Face à elle, une toile de plus deux mètres. Je regarde Adèle se lancer dans la réalisation du *Gutter Paradise #11* et je suis frappé par son envie et sa détermination. C'est l'expression même de la peinture totale que nous voulons tous défendre. Il faut voir Adèle Renault en action, comme tant d'autres, pour s'imprégner de cette vibration. Une force que seule procure la peinture, sous toutes ses formes.

De ses premières études sur les pigeons, à la minutie du détail des plumes, Adèle Renault a mûri cette nouvelle série, ce paradis mis en scène à partir de rien ; celui d'un détail devenu le sujet.

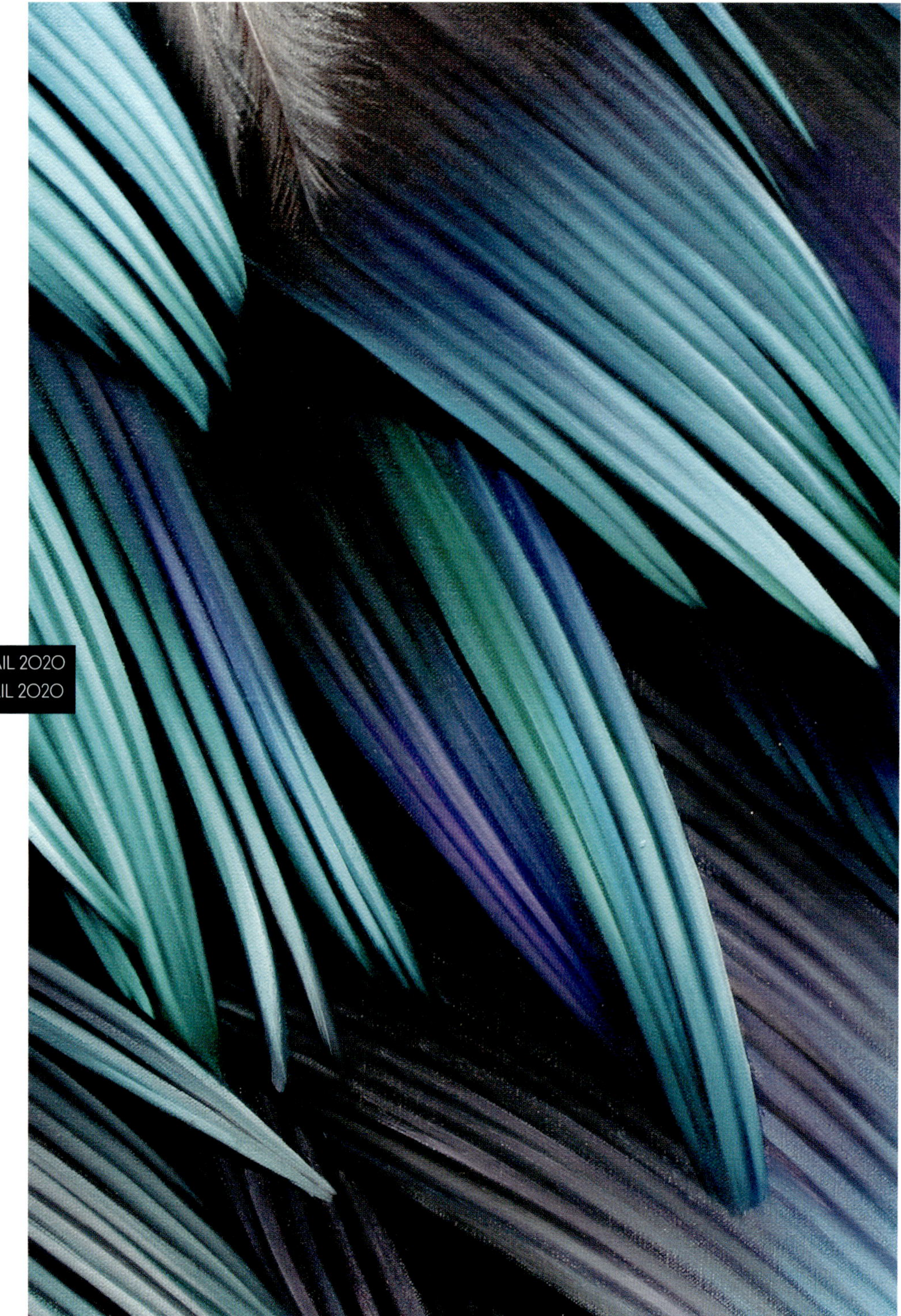

OIL PAINTING DETAIL 2O2O
SPRAY PAINT DETAIL 2O2O

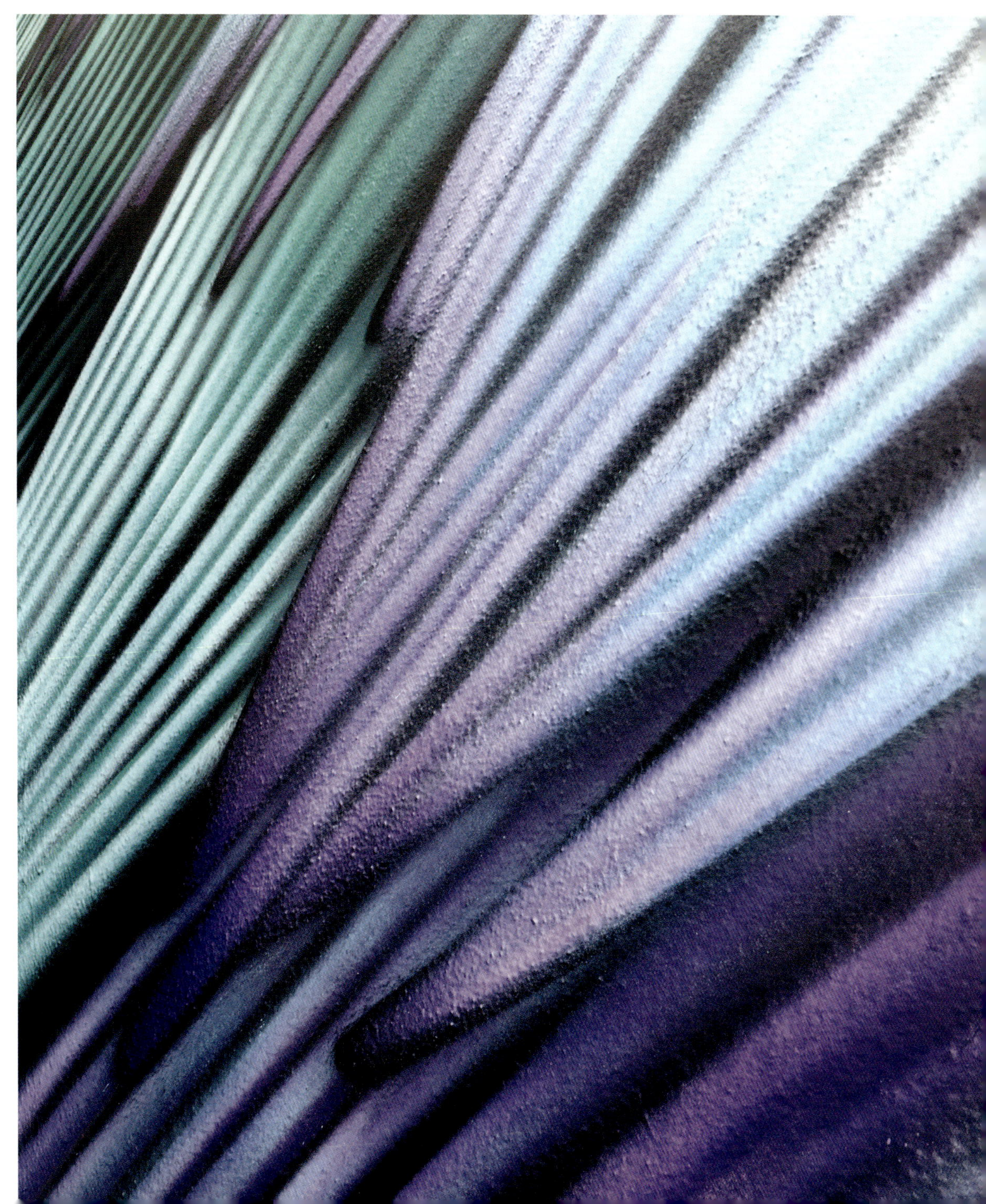

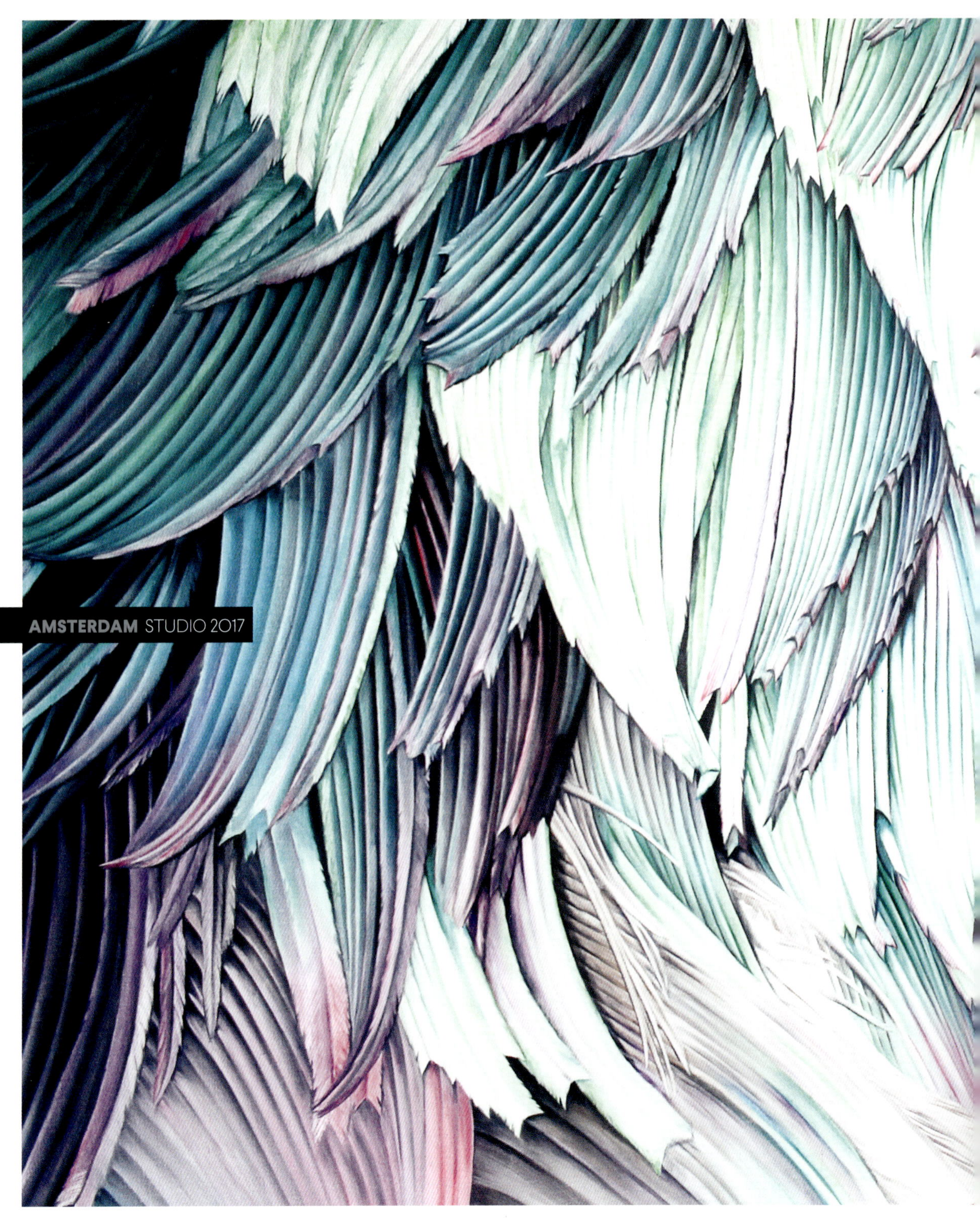

AMSTERDAM STUDIO 2017

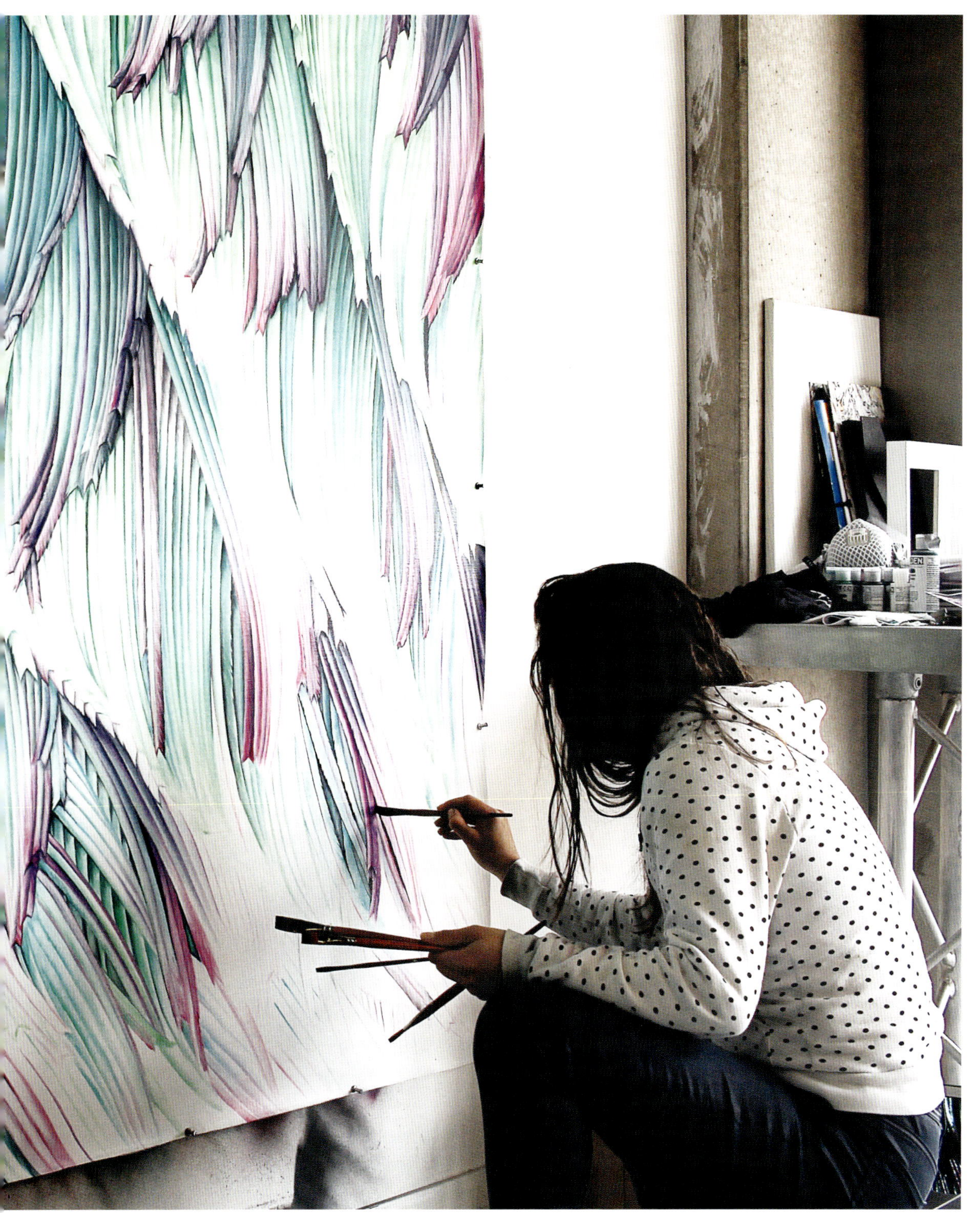

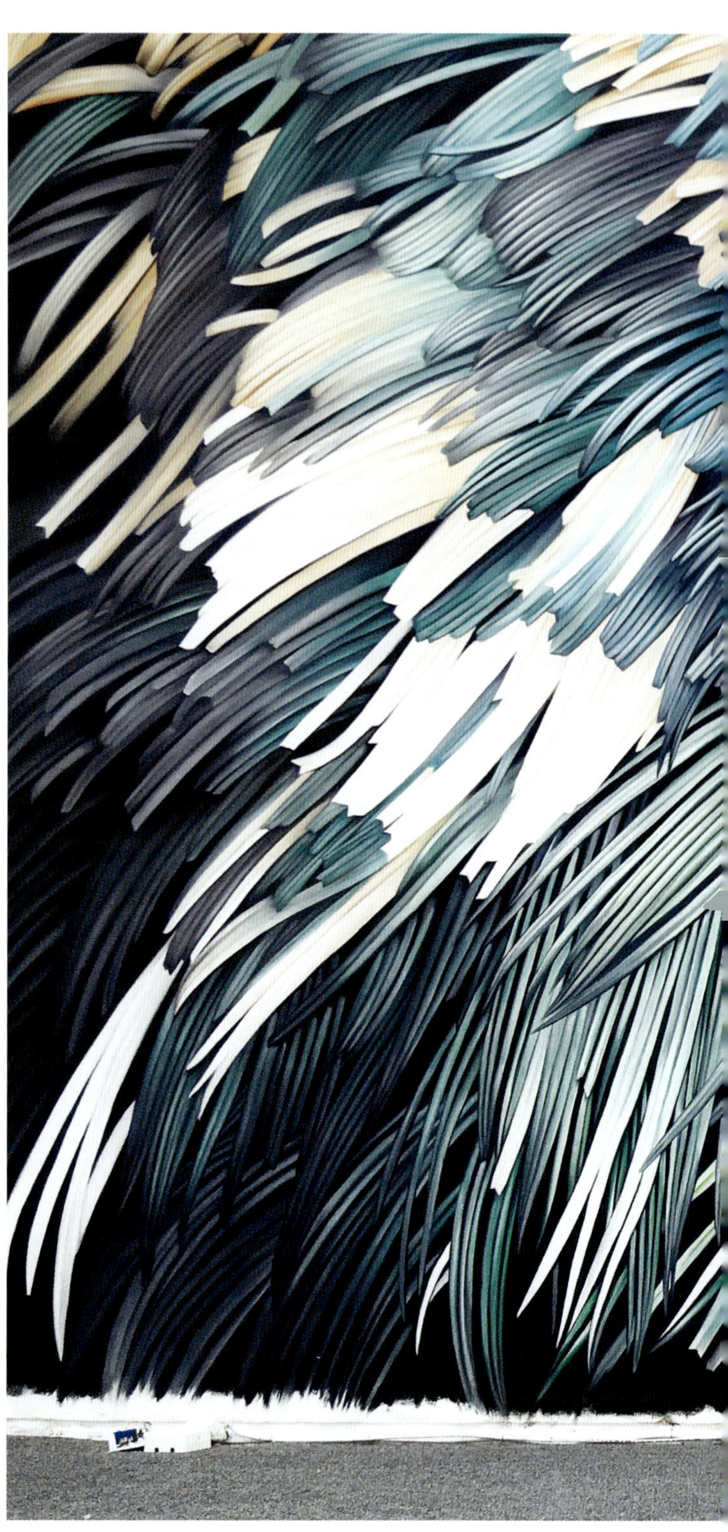

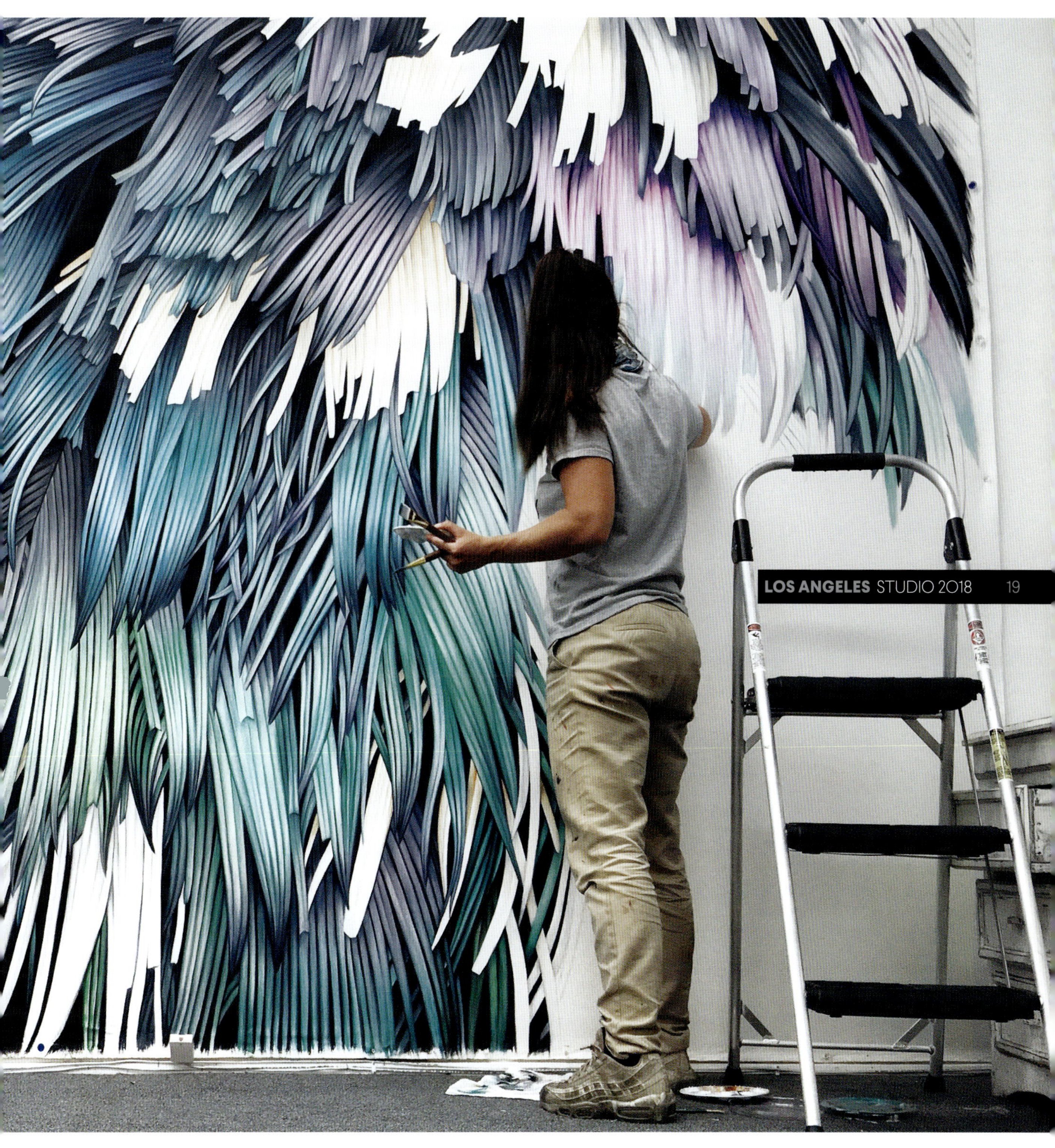
LOS ANGELES STUDIO 2018   19

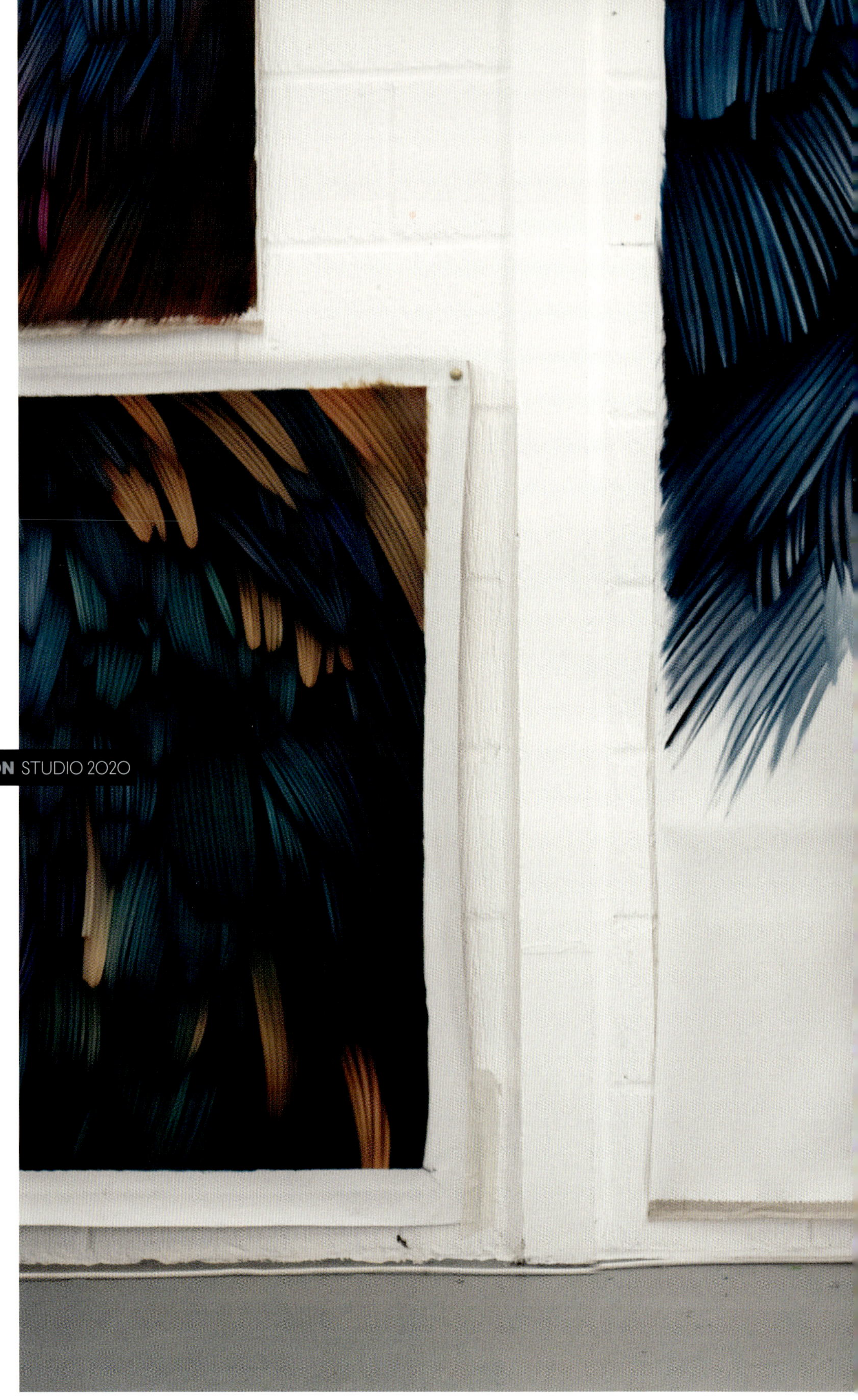

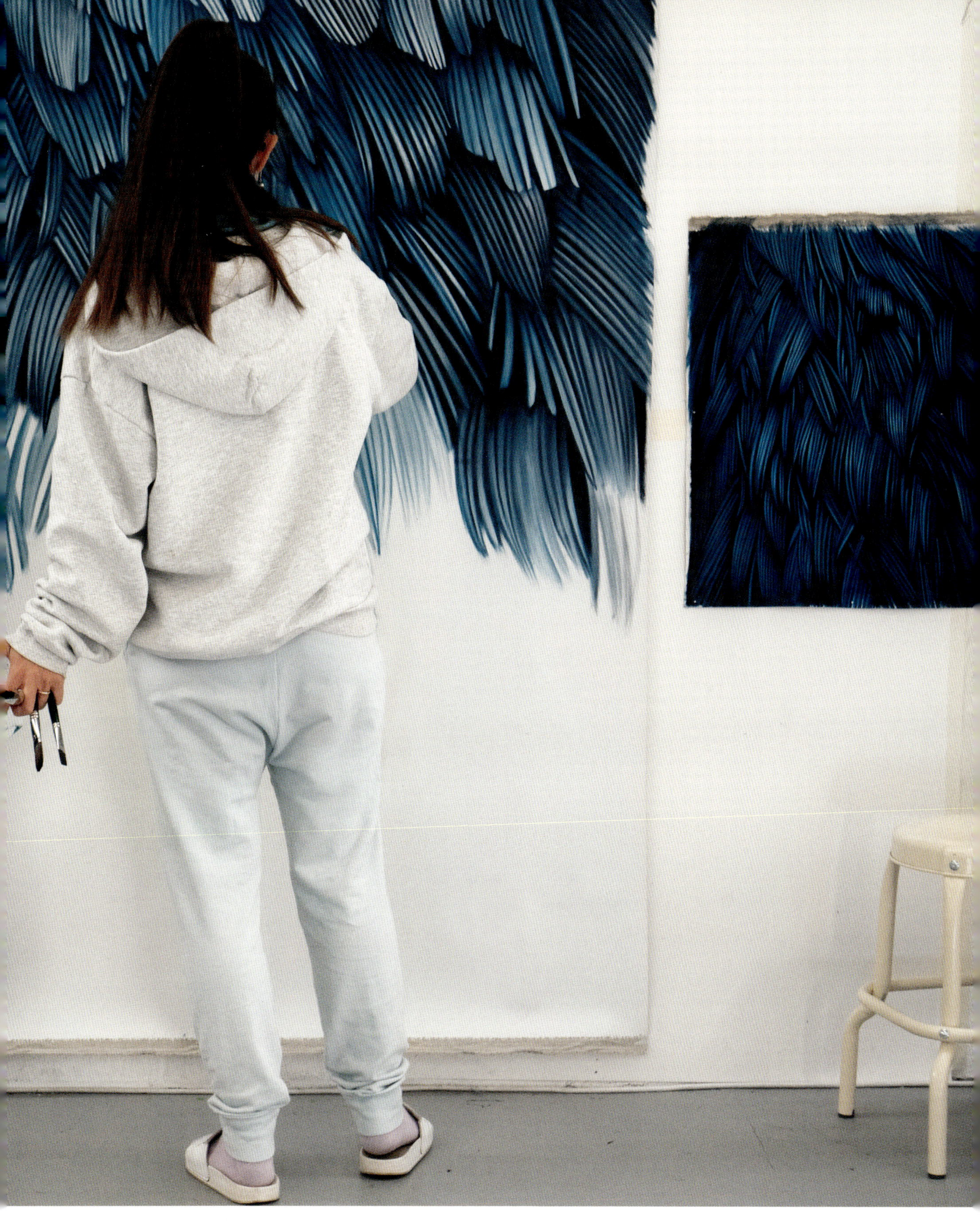

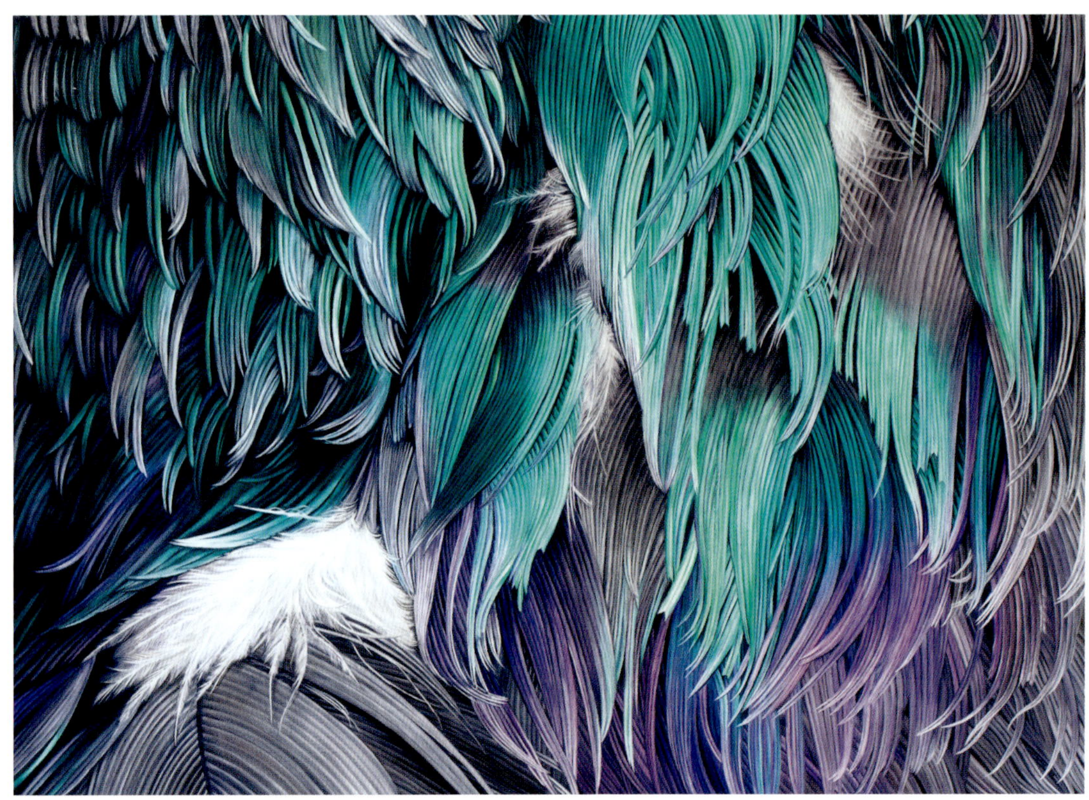

Gutter Paradise #2

2016 | oil on linen | 140 x 100 cm

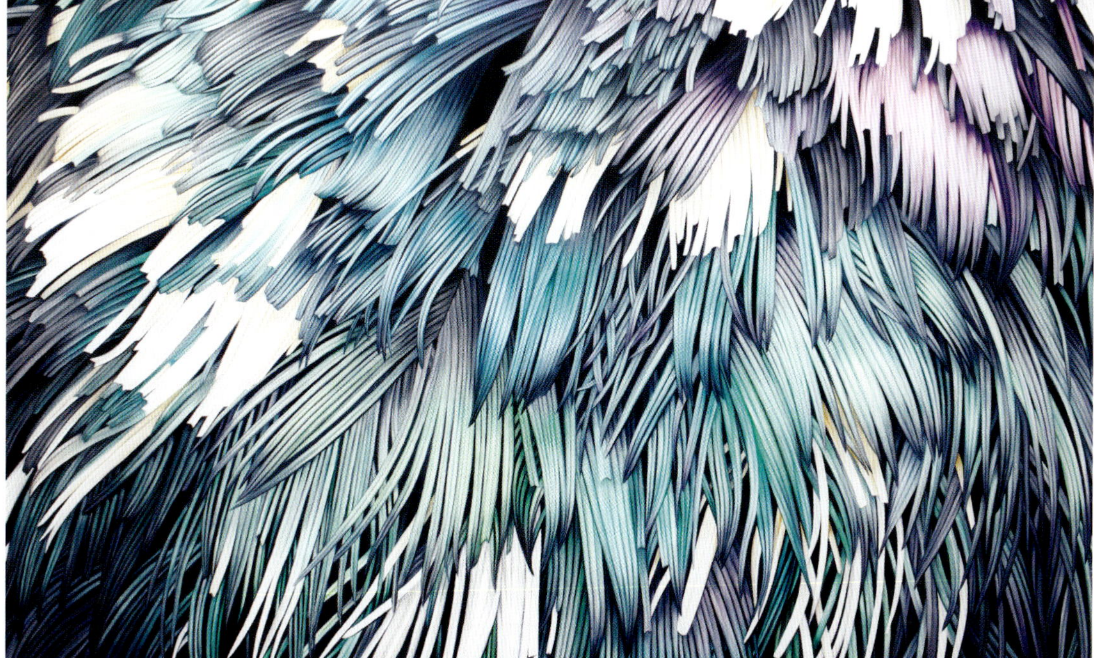

Gutter Paradise #8

2018 | oil on linen | 260 x 180 cm

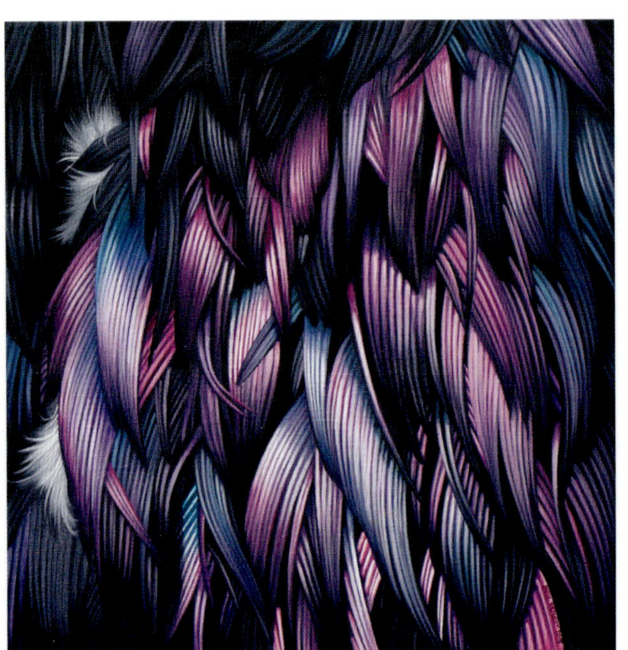

Gutter Paradise #7

2018 | oil on linen | 30 x 30 cm

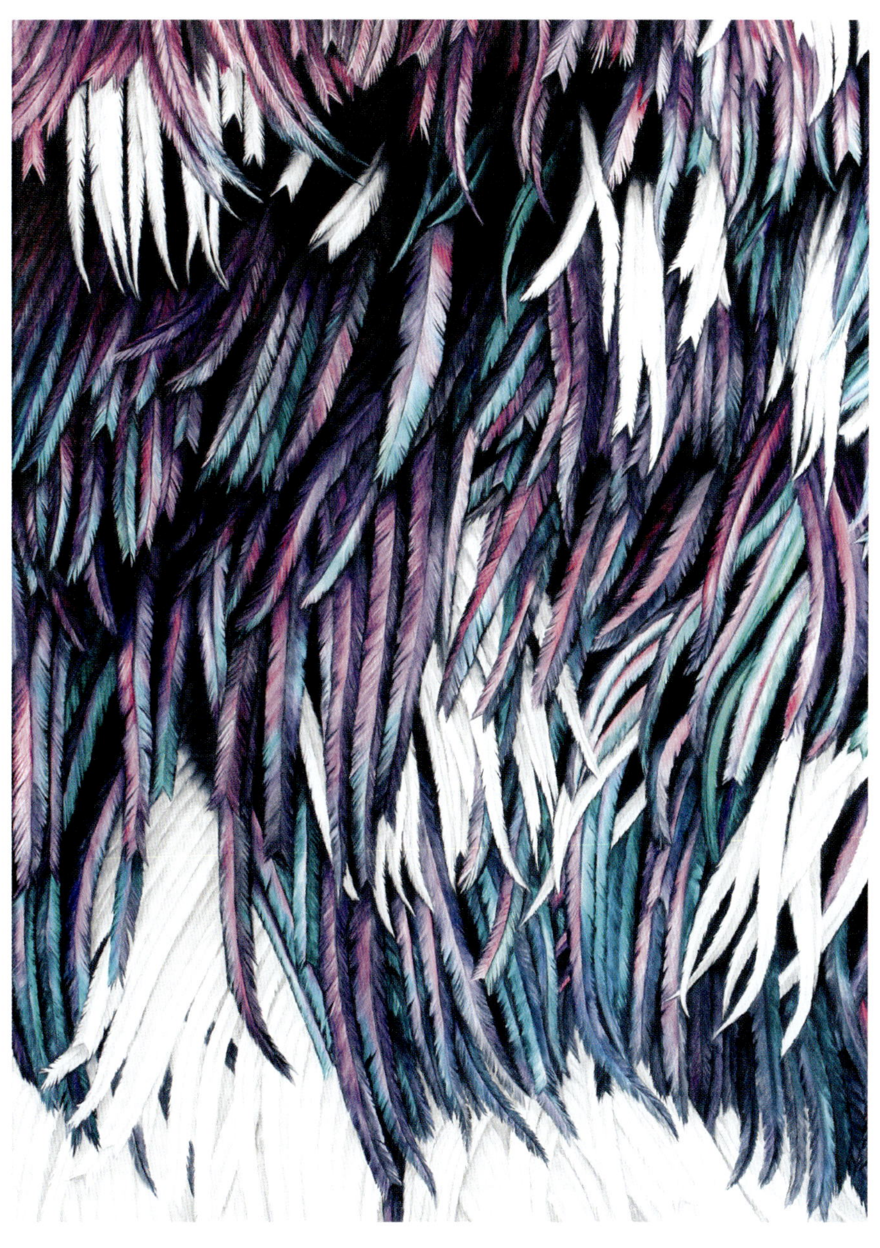

Gutter Paradise #4

2016 | oil on linen | 60 x 80 cm

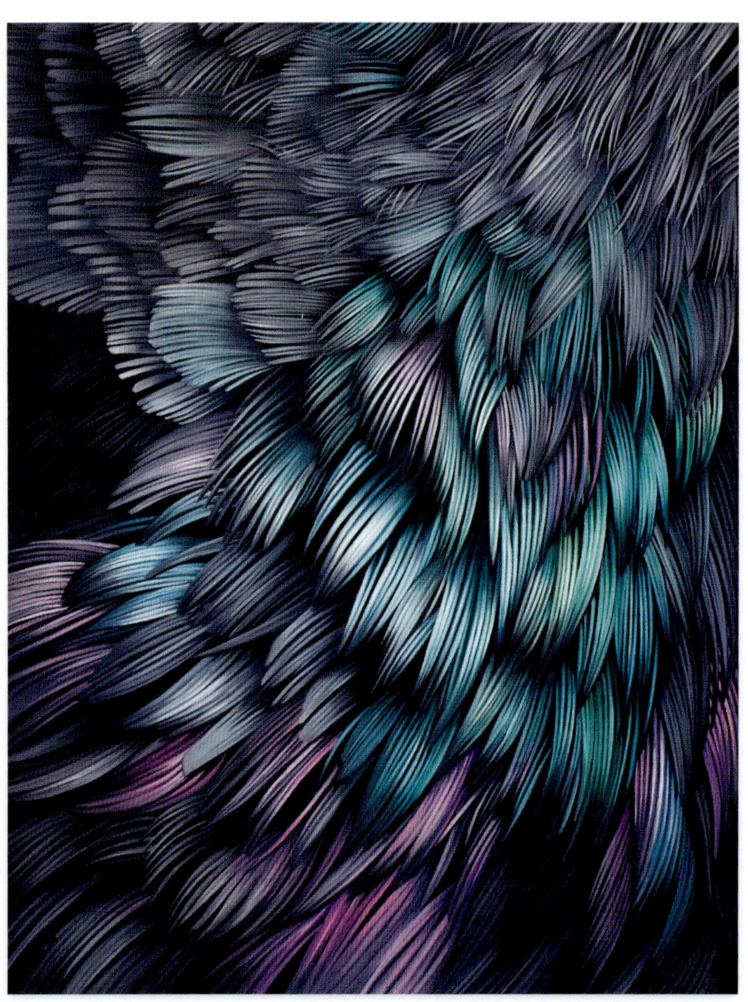

Gutter Paradise #12

2019 | oil on linen | 40 x 50 cm

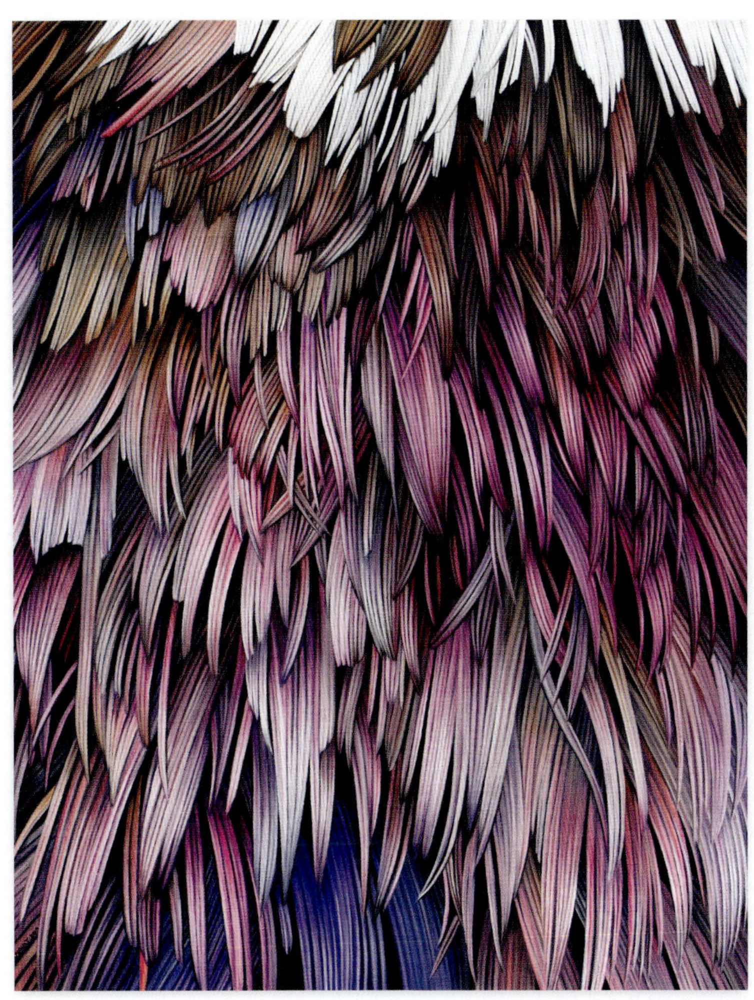

Gutter Paradise #9

2019 | oil on linen | 40 x 50 cm

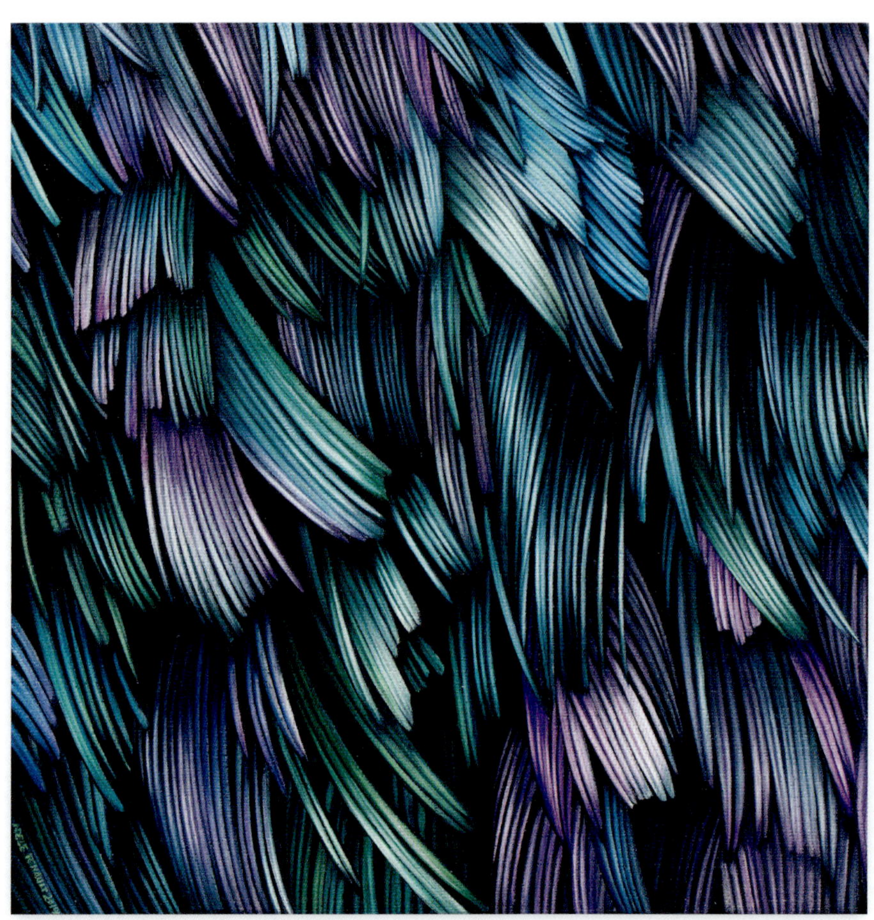

Gutter Paradise #10

2019 | oil on linen | 25 x 25 cm

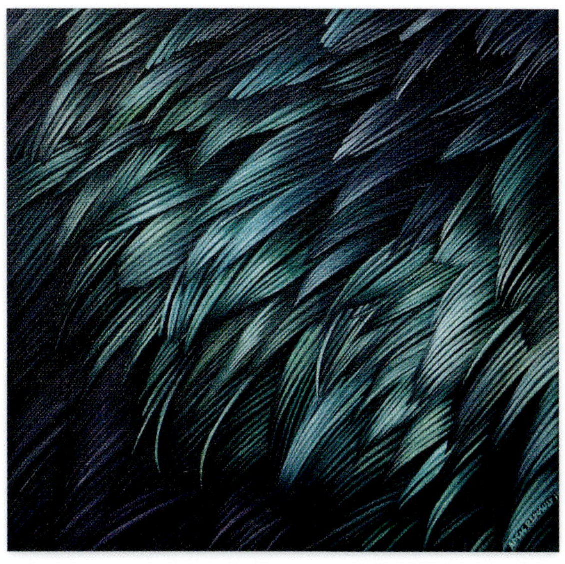

Gutter Paradise #13

2019 | oil on linen | 20 x 20cm

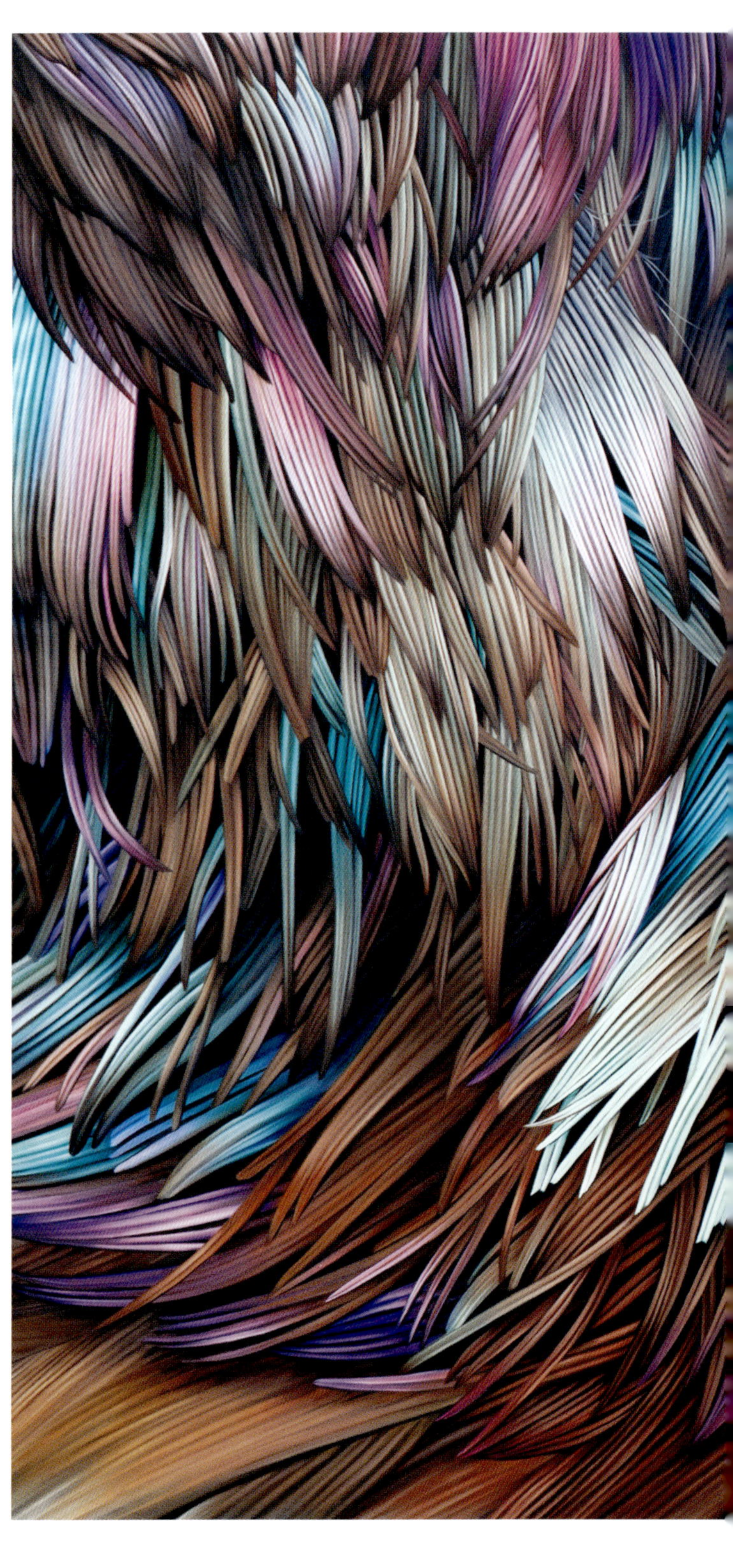

Gutter Paradise #11

2019 | oil on linen | 270 x 200 cm

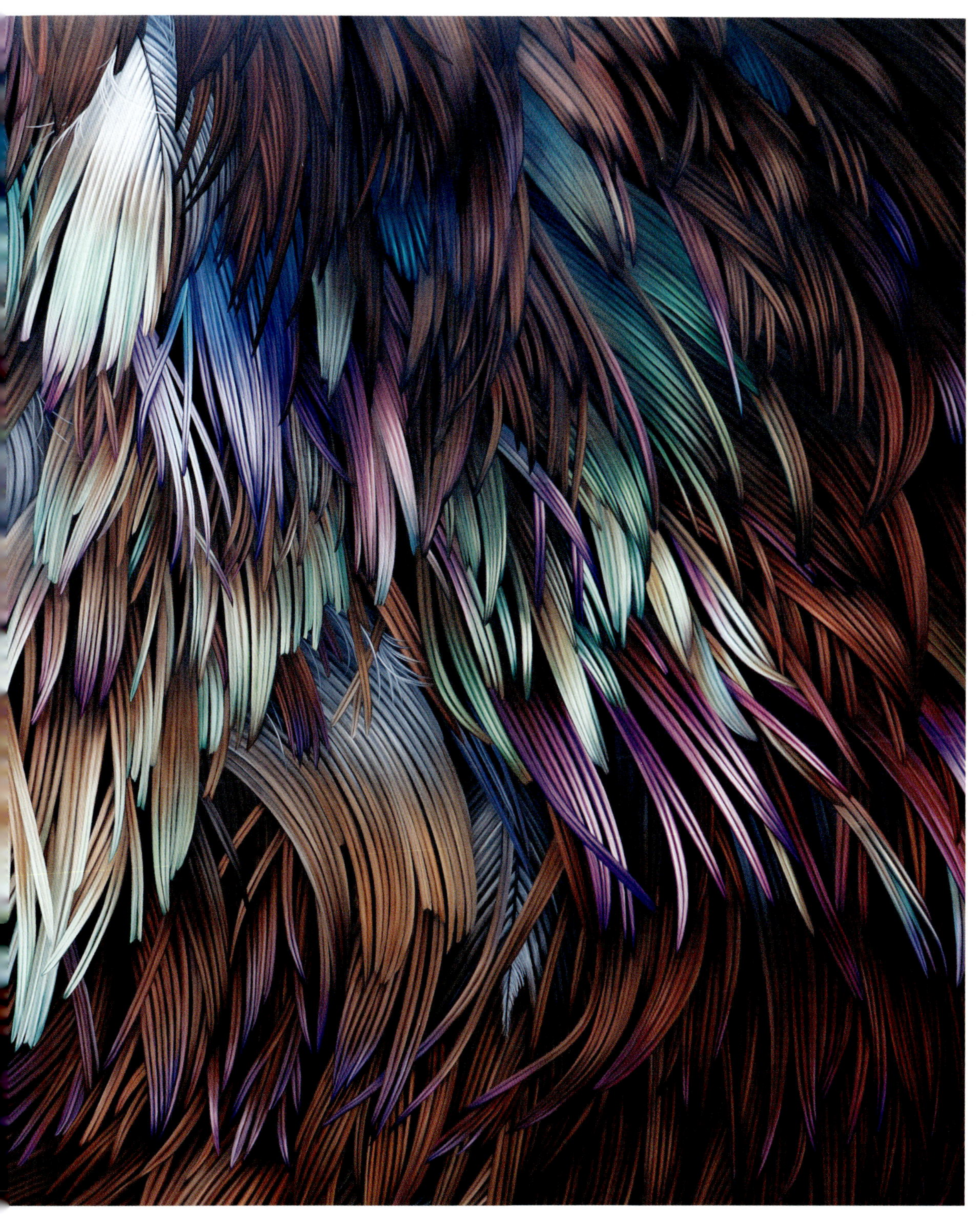

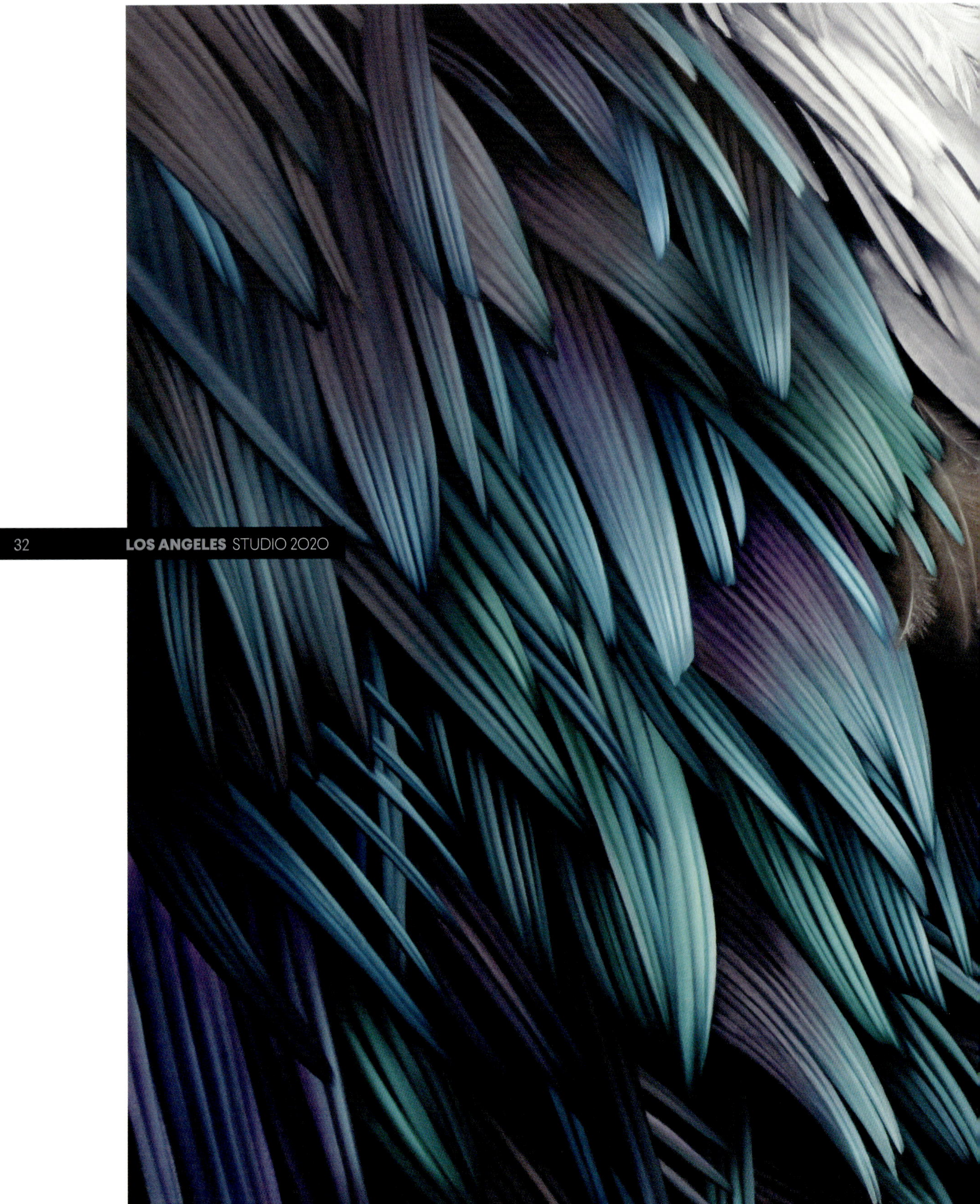

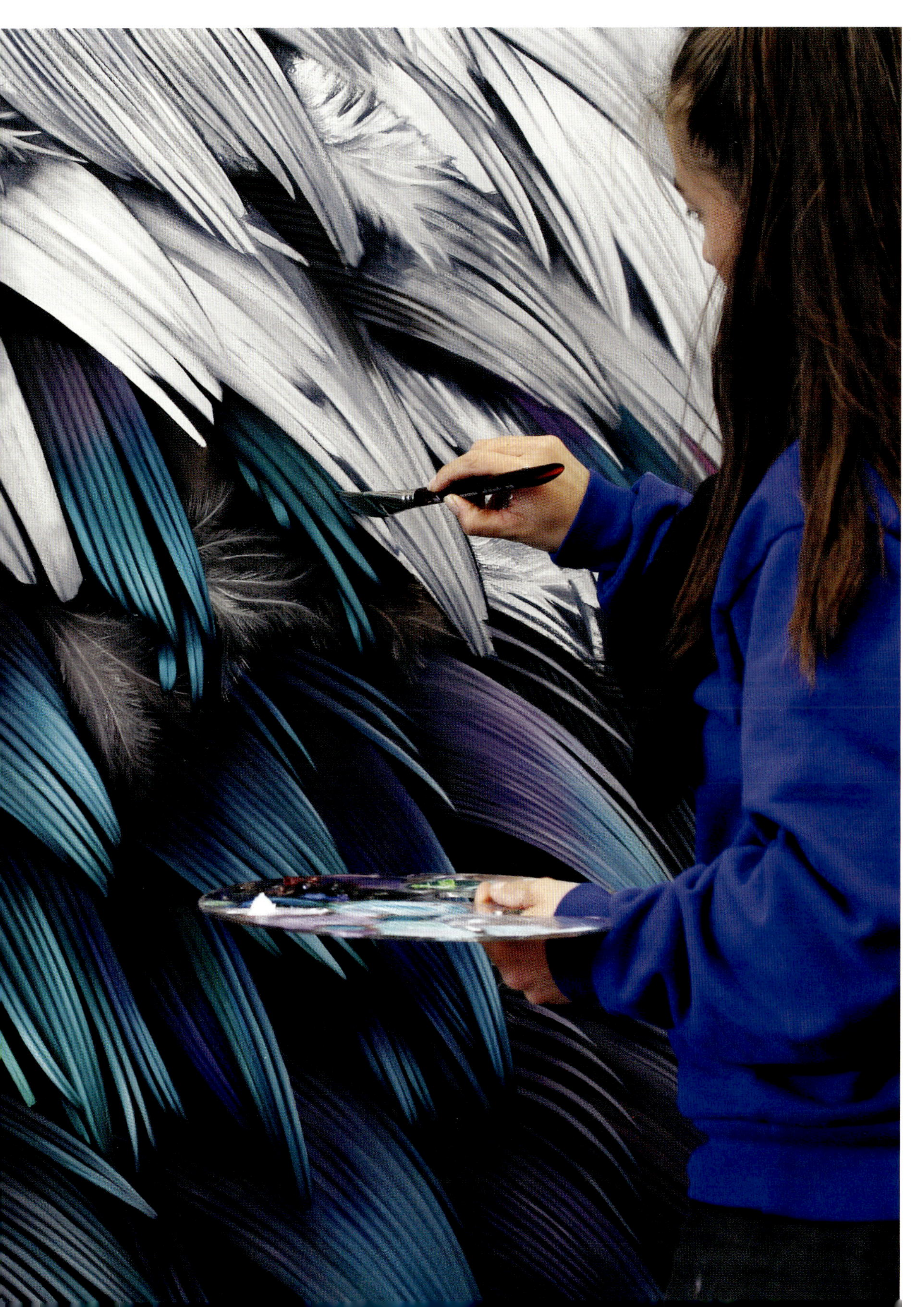

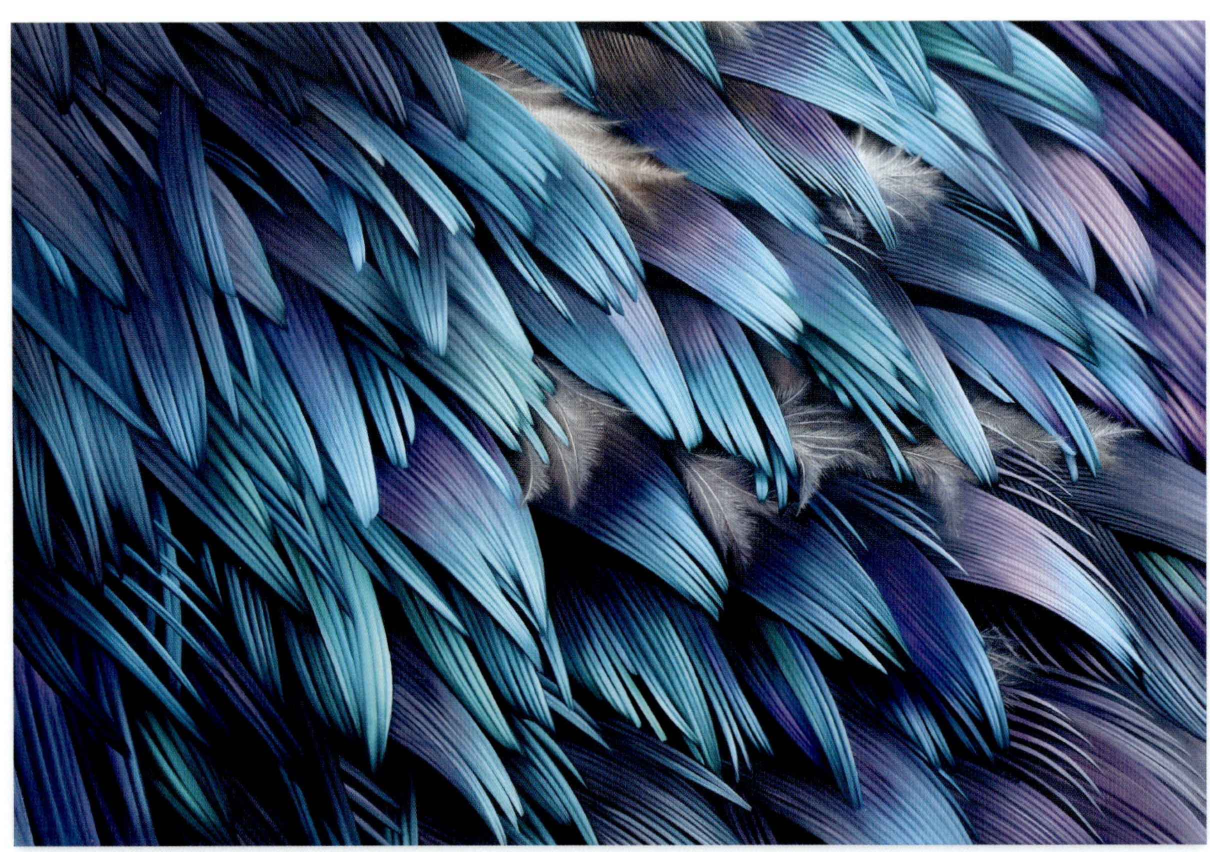

Gutter Paradise #14

2020 | oil on linen | 130 x 95 cm

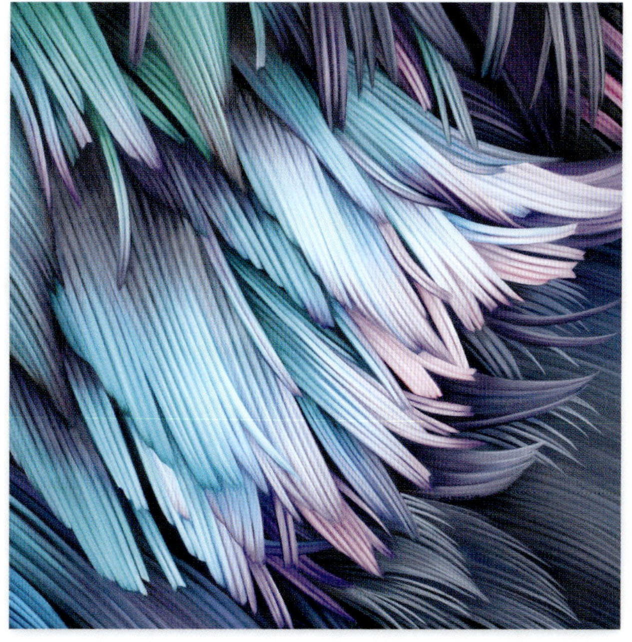

Gutter Paradise #16

2020 | oil on linen | 45 x 45 cm

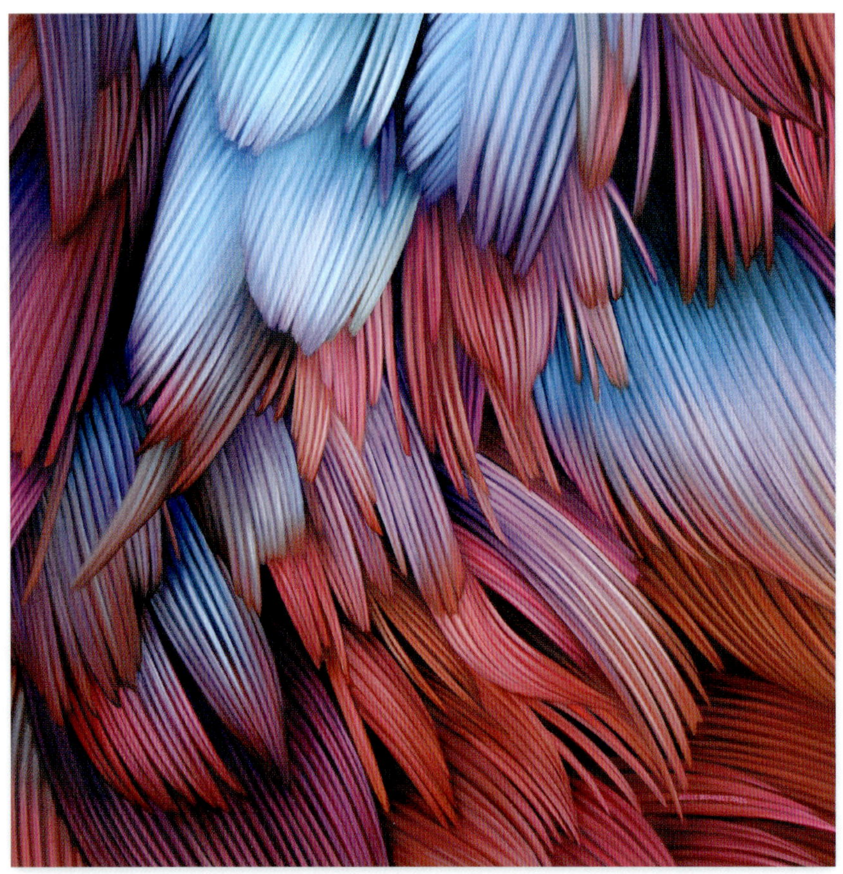

Gutter Paradise #16

2020 | oil on linen | 45 x 45 cm

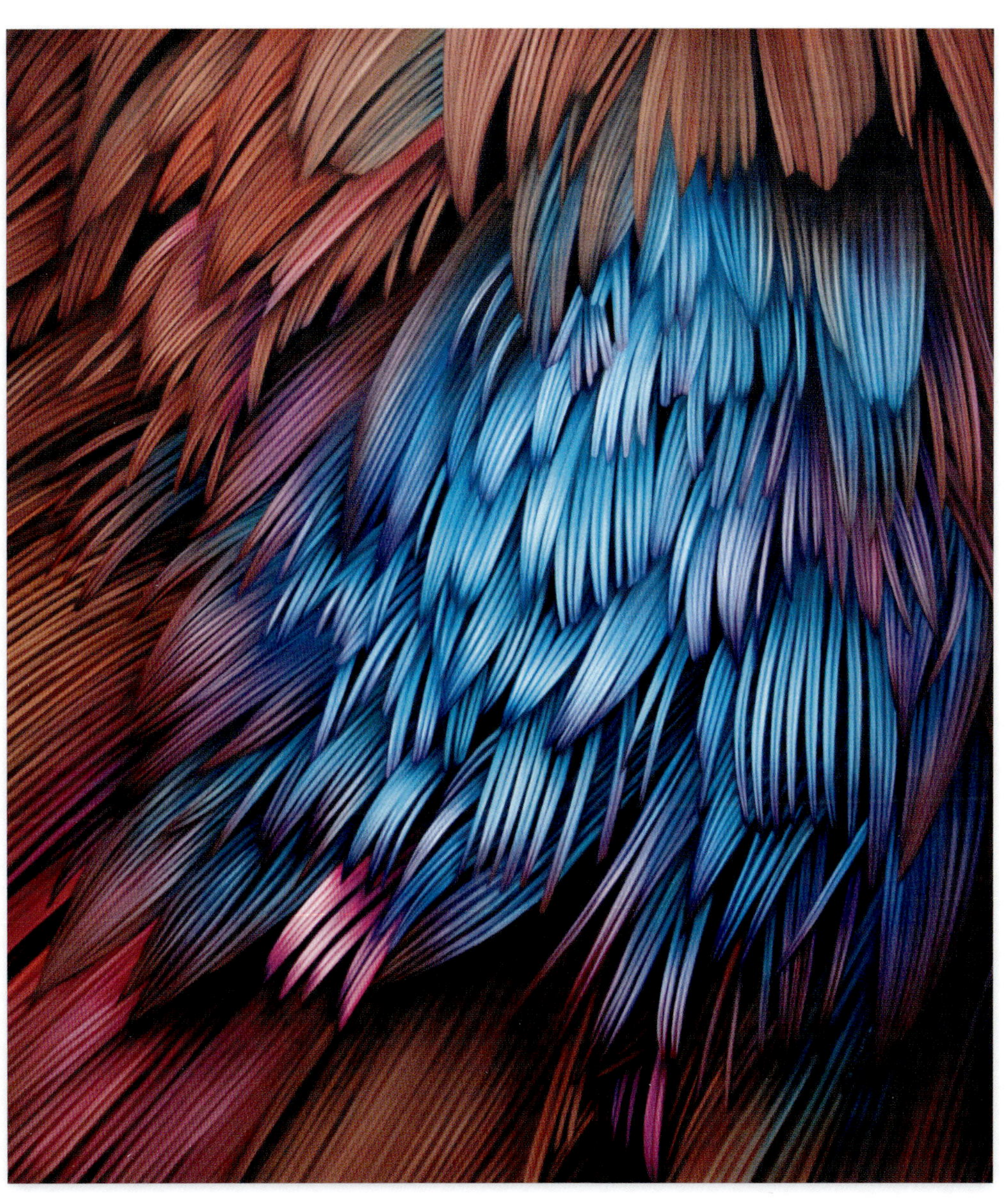

Gutter Paradise #18

2020 | oil on linen | 75 x 95 cm

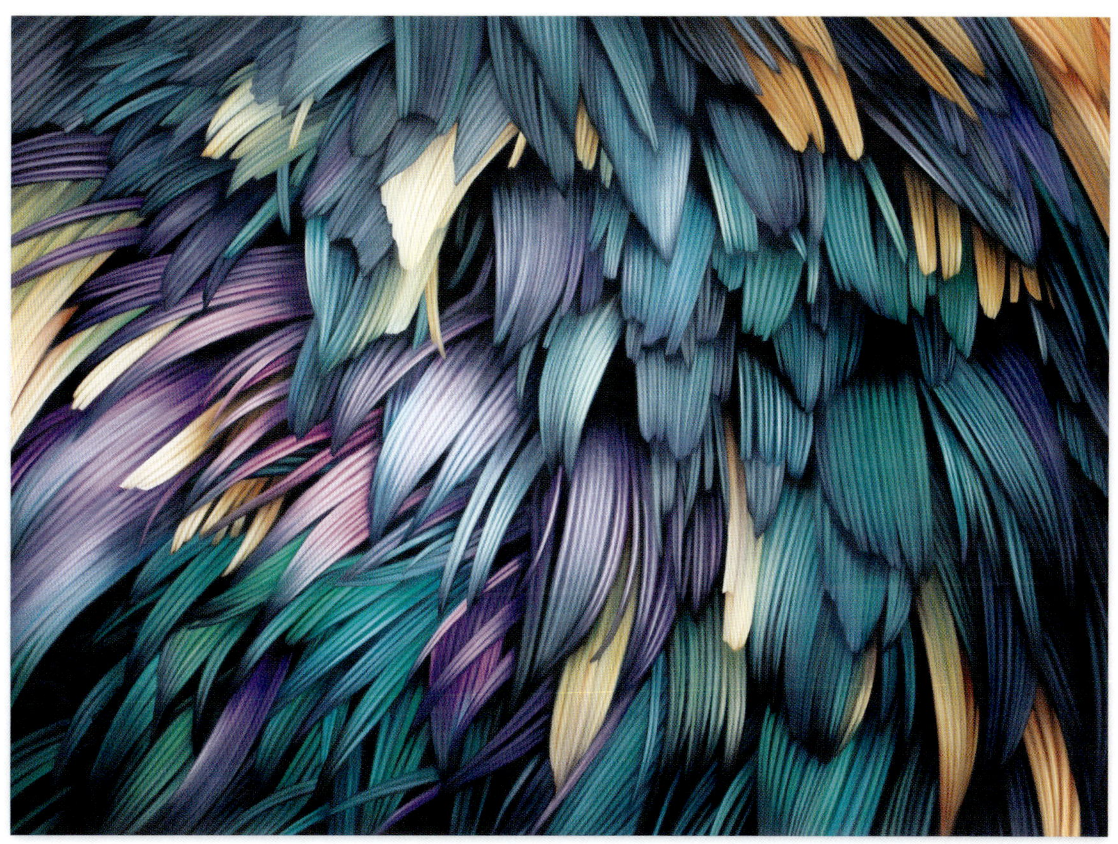

Gutter Paradise #17

2020 | oil on linen | 130 x 95 cm

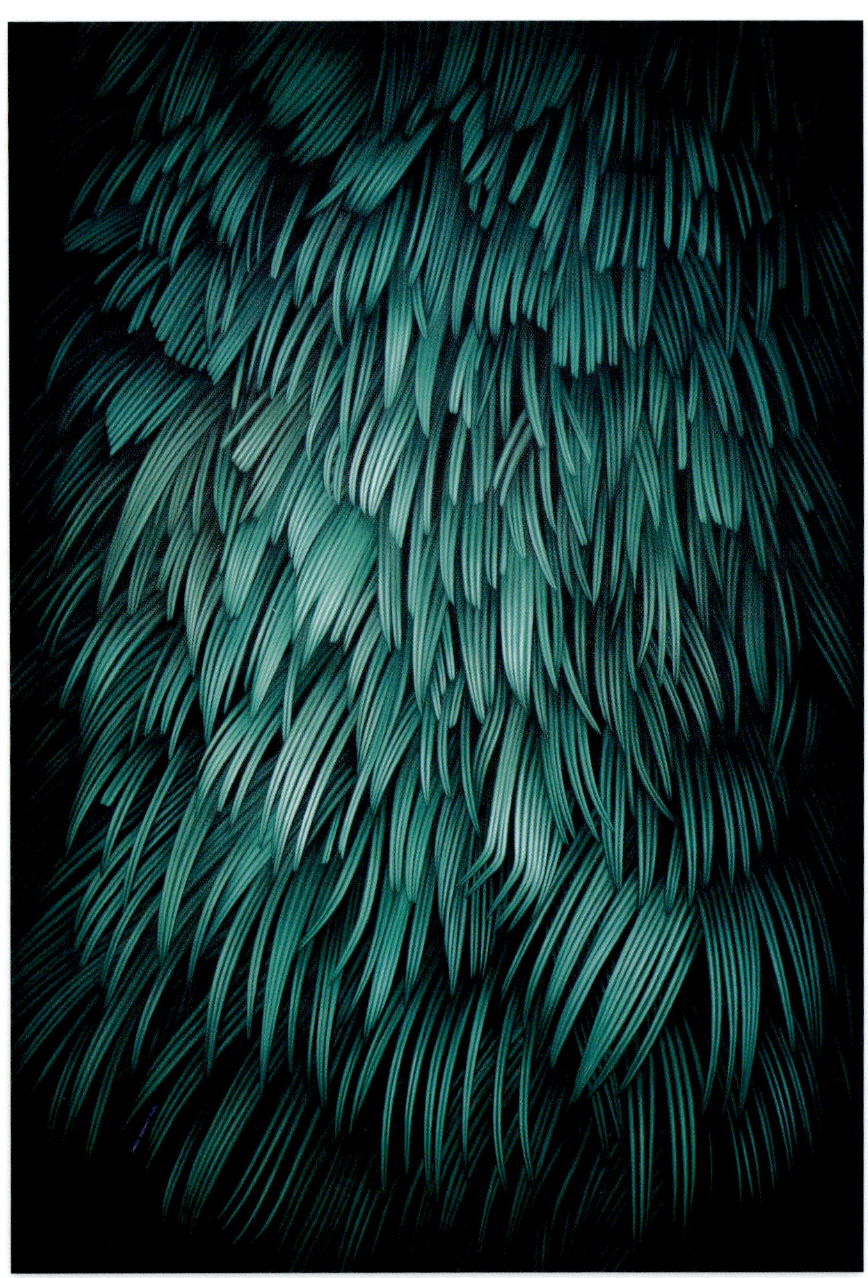

Bluebells #1 (diptych)

2020 | oil on linen | 130 x 200 cm

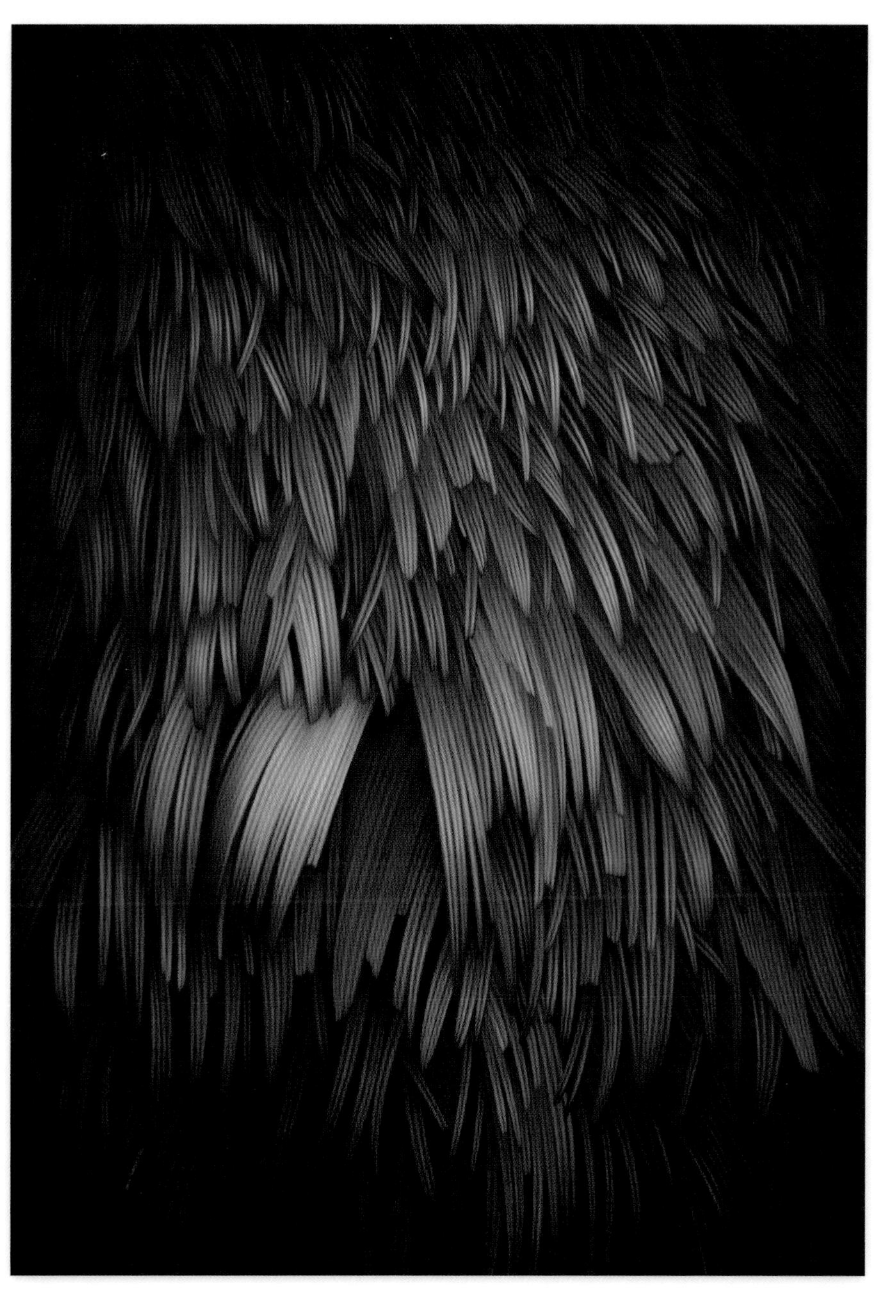

Bluebells #2 (diptych)
2020 | oil on linen | 130 x 200 cm

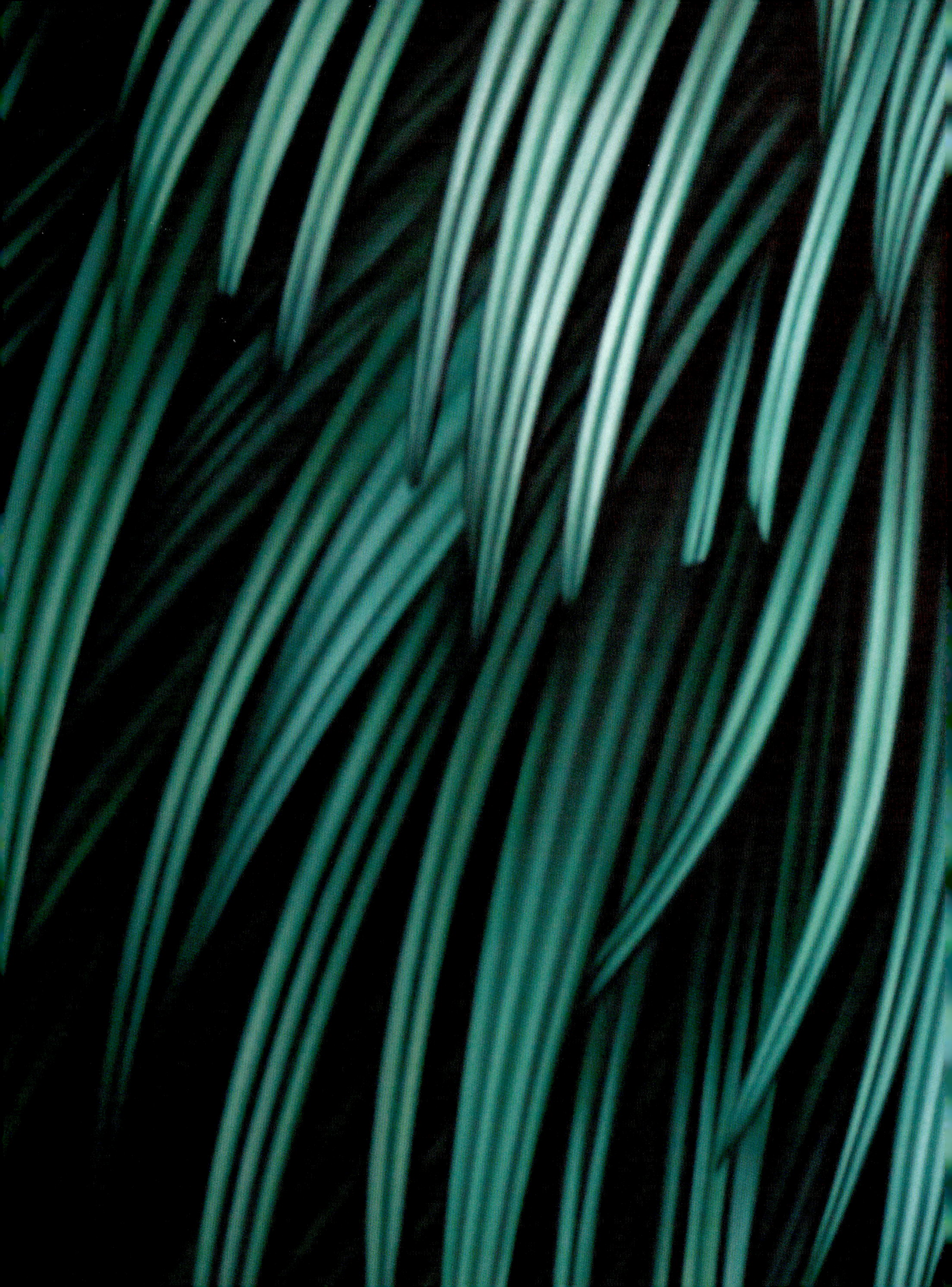

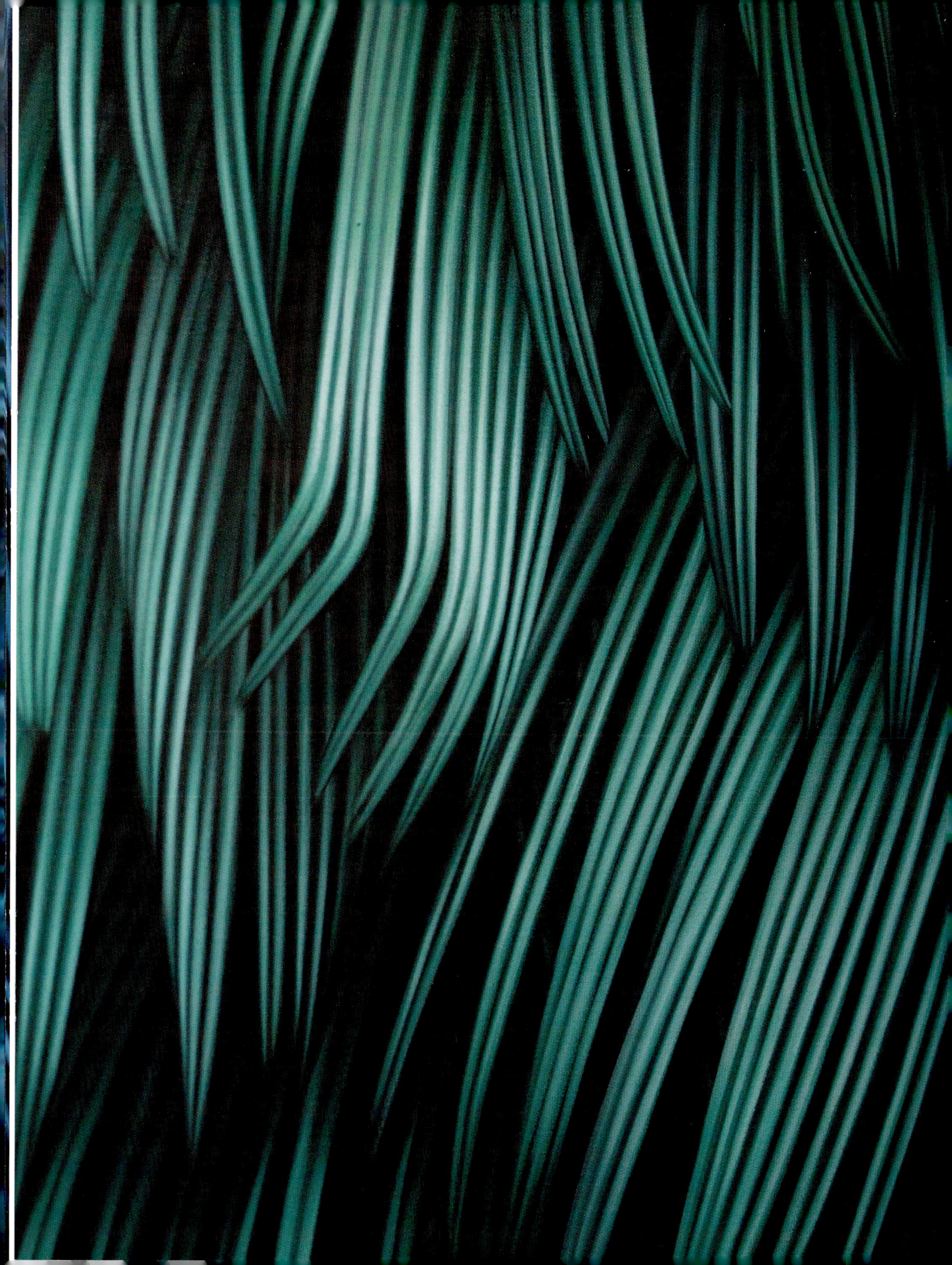

Black Matter

2020 | oil on linen | 80 x 120 cm

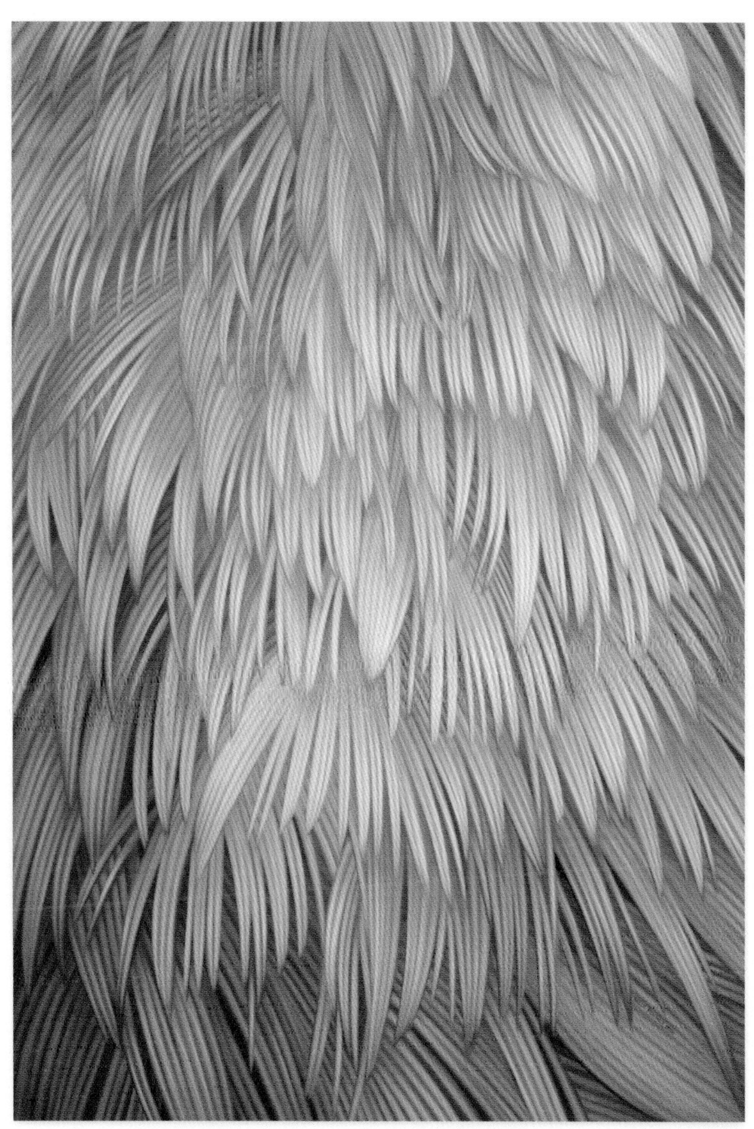

Grey Matter
2020 | oil on linen | 80 x 120 cm

Candy Socks

2020 | oil on linen | 90 x 120 cm

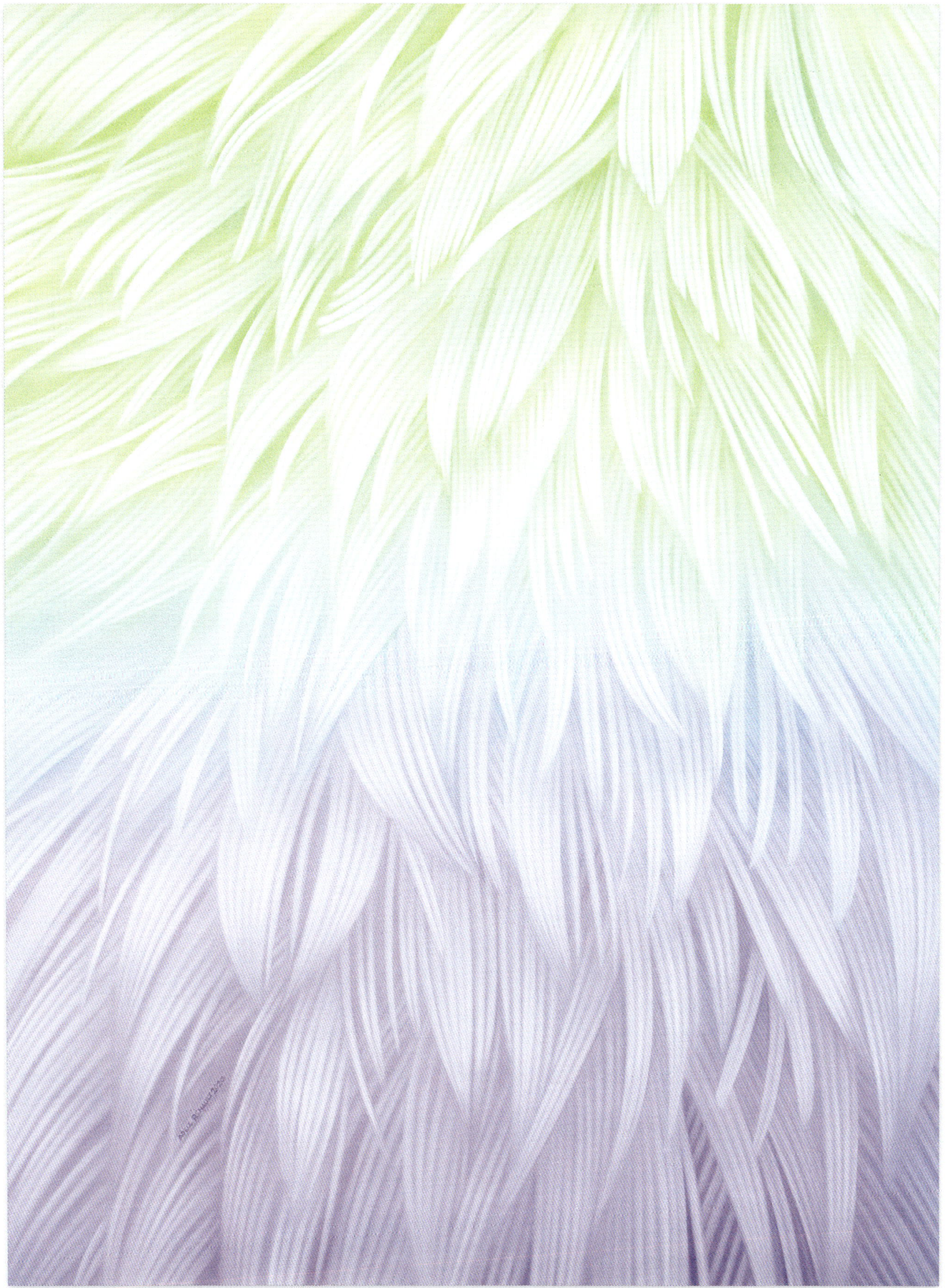

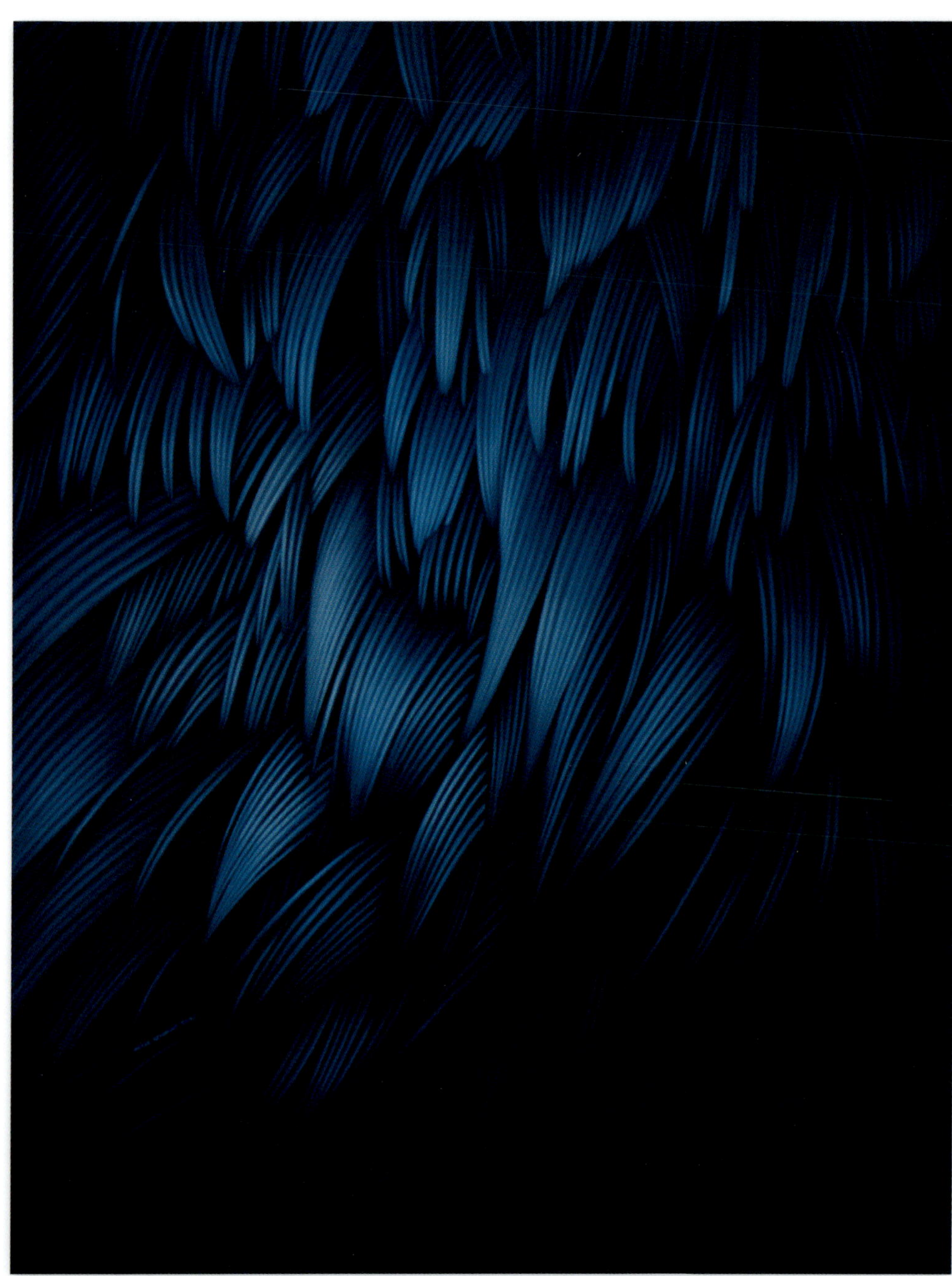

Blue Monday
2020 | oil on linen | 90 x 120 cm

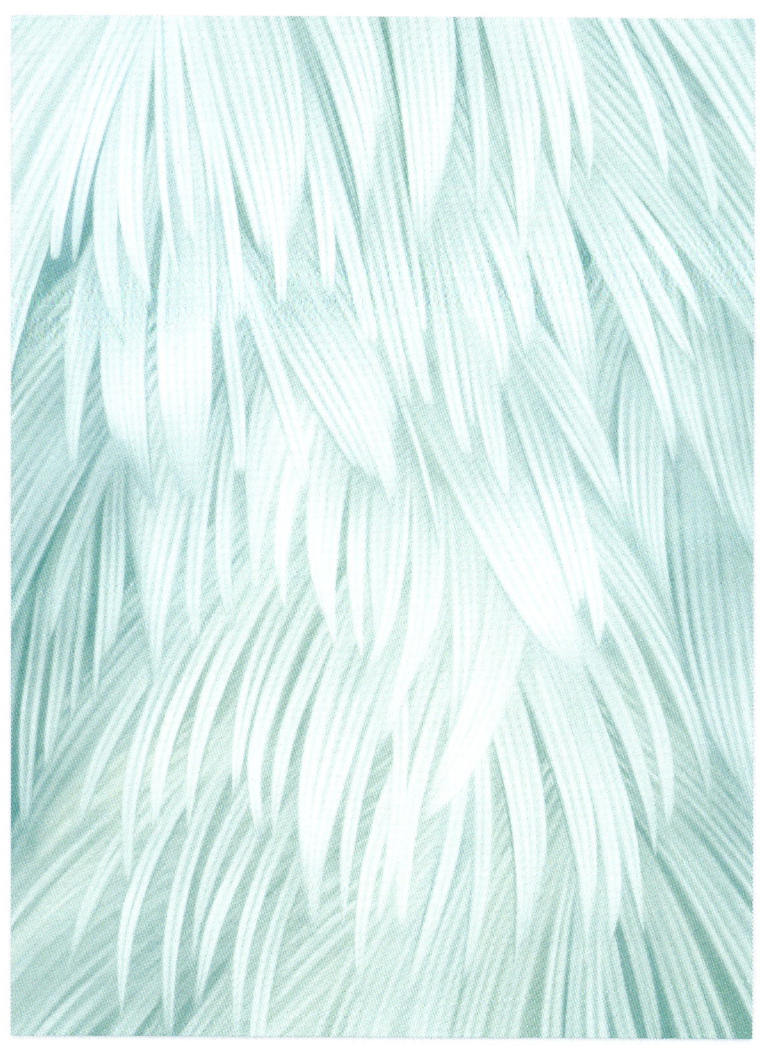

Paris Metro

2020 | oil on linen | 65 x 85 cm

MURALS

Fresques

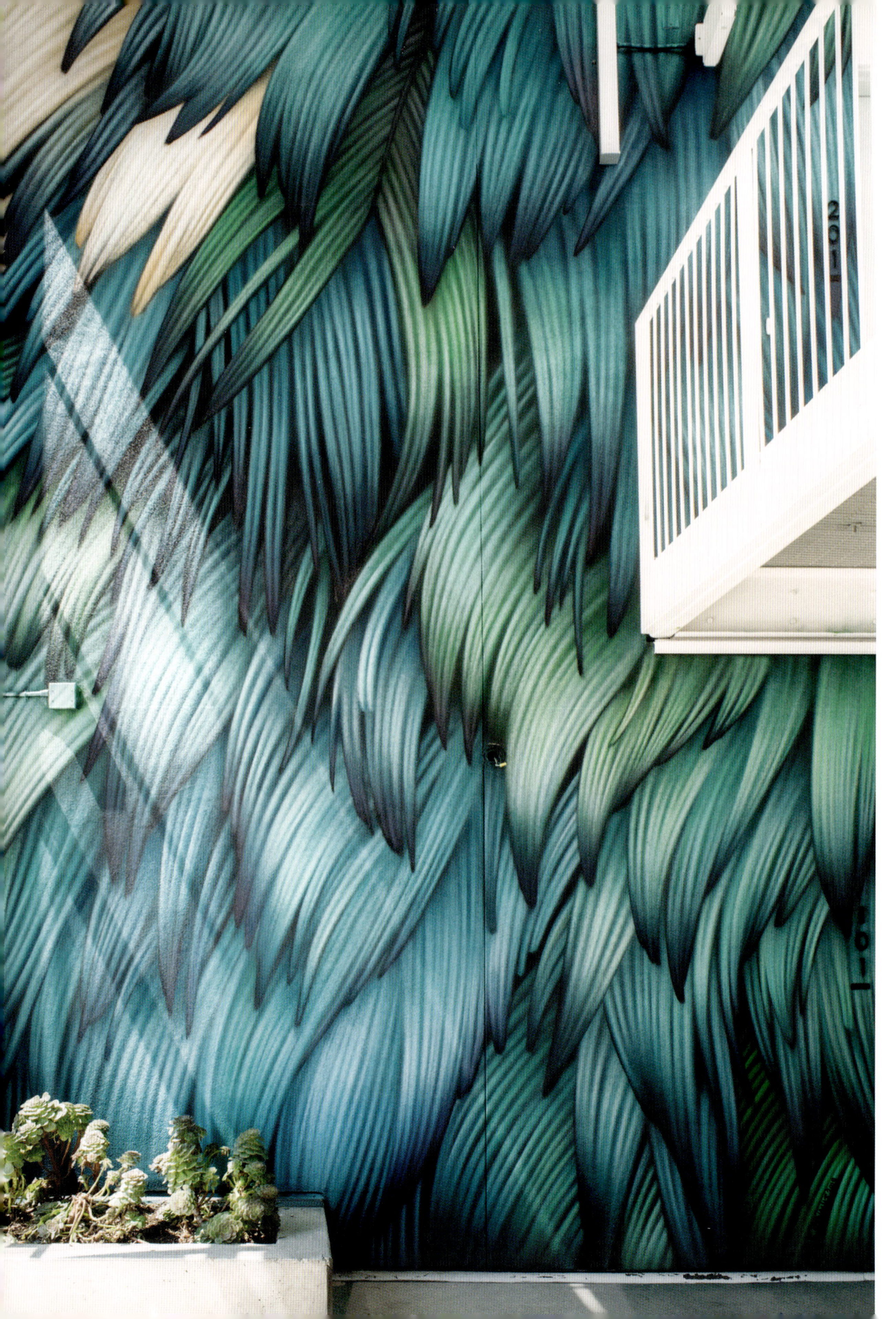

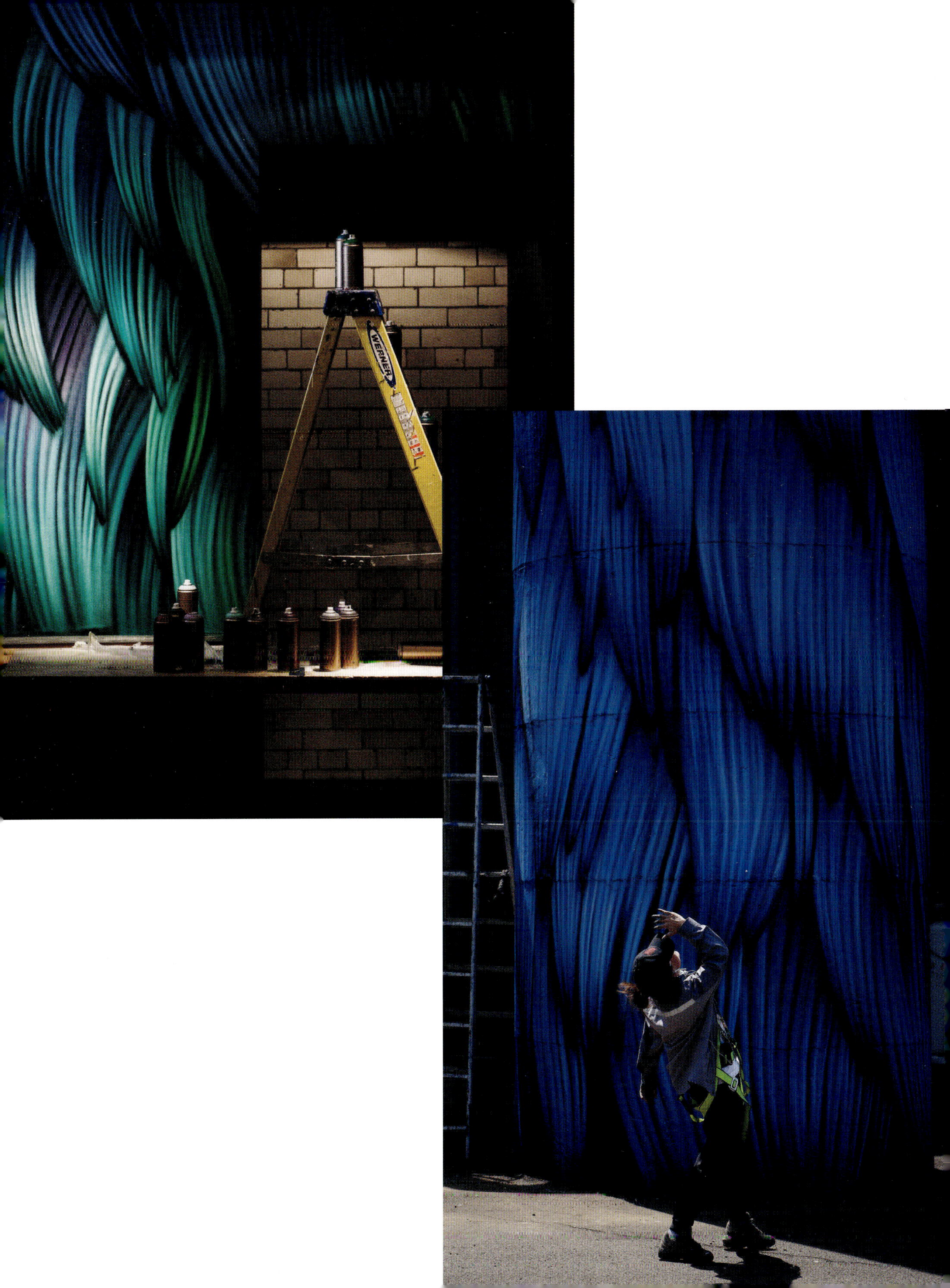

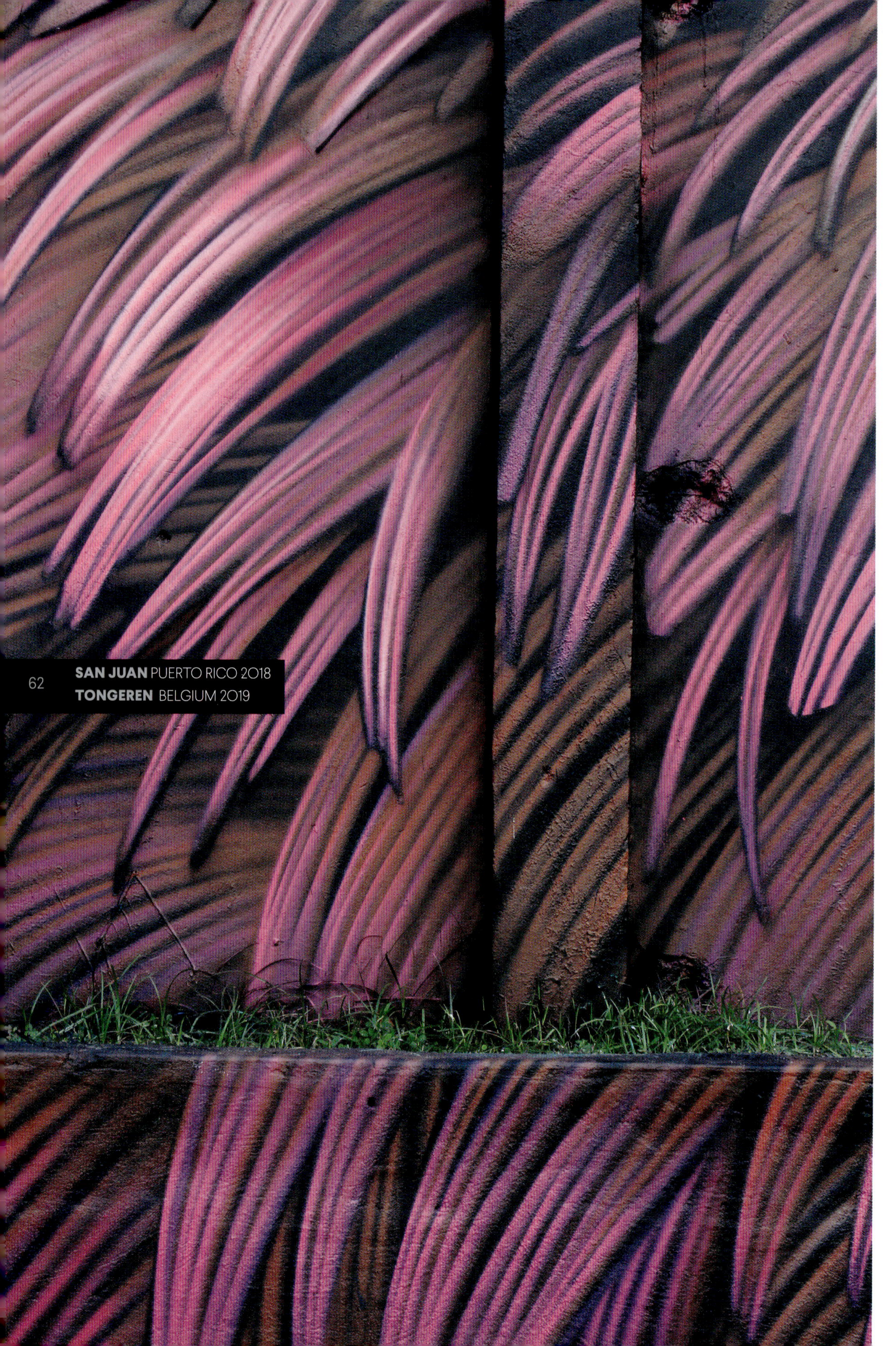

SAN JUAN PUERTO RICO 2018
TONGEREN BELGIUM 2019

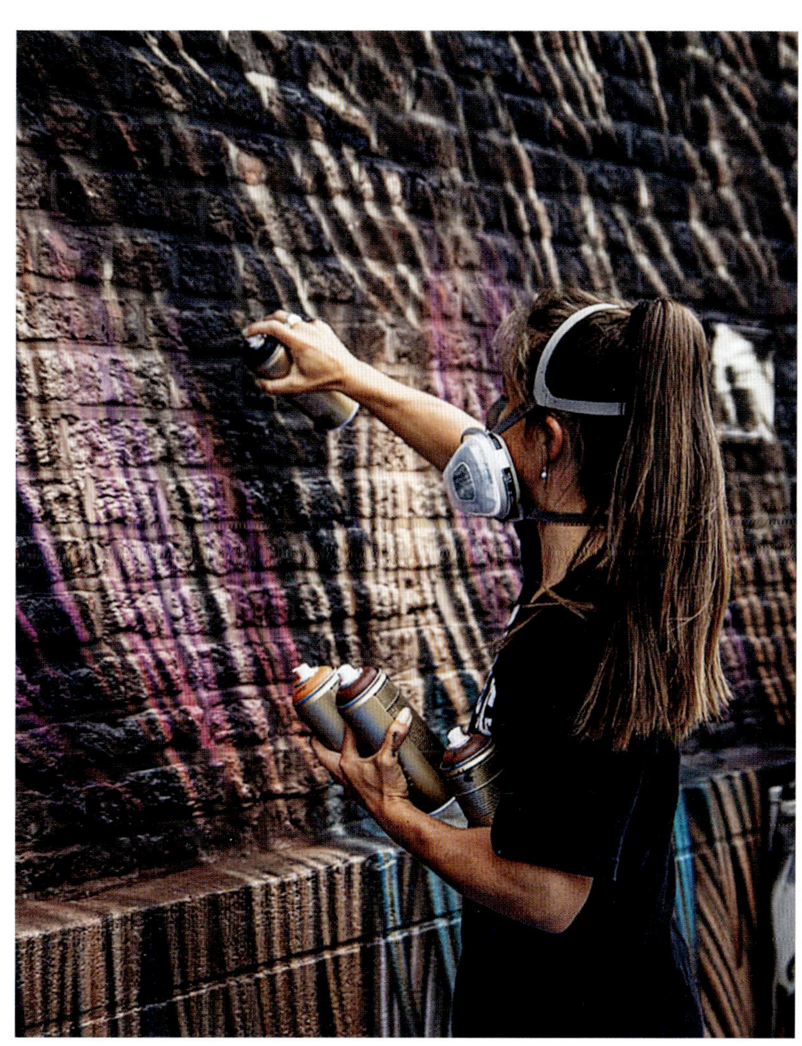

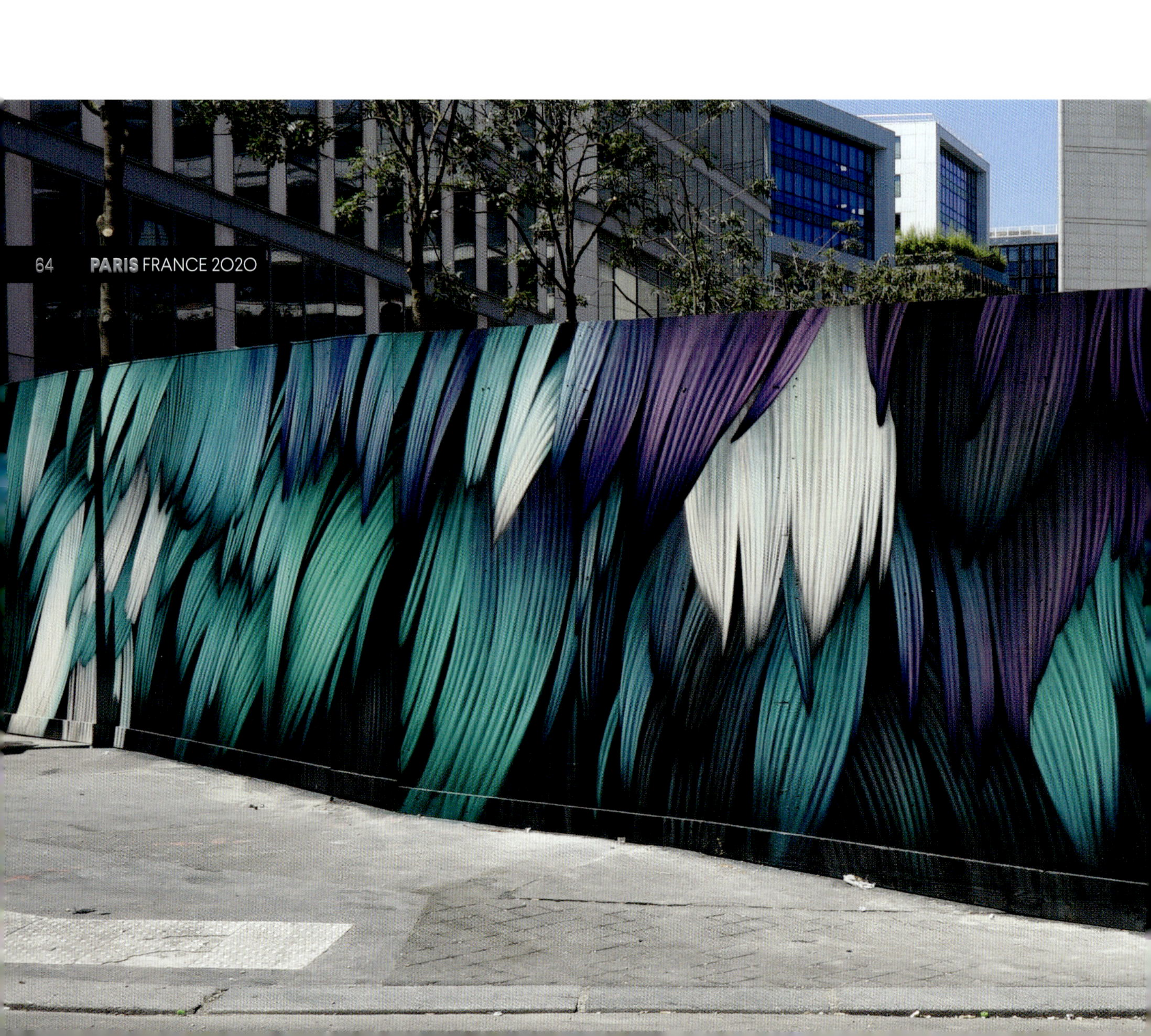

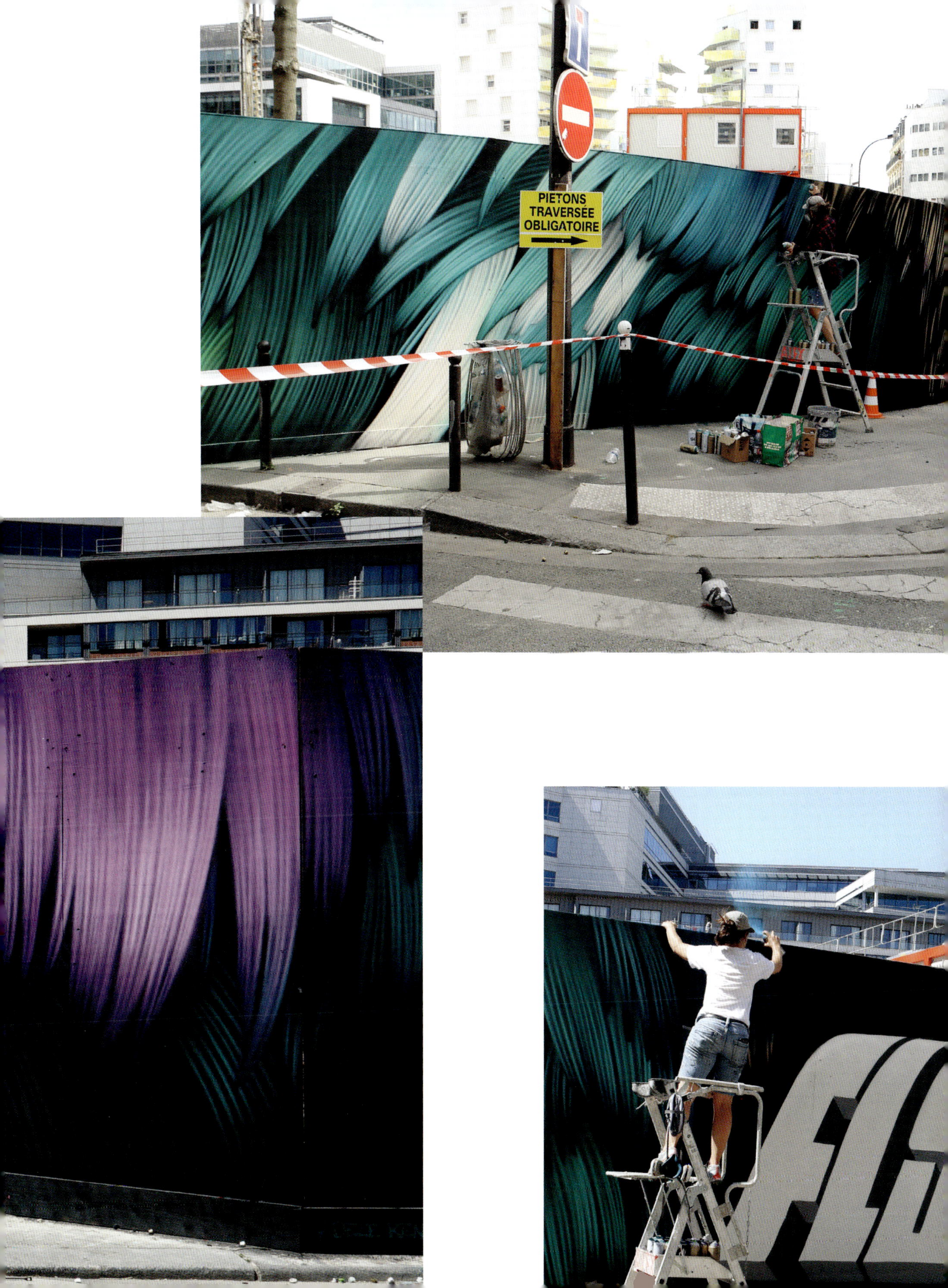

PIÉTONS
TRAVERSÉE
OBLIGATOIRE

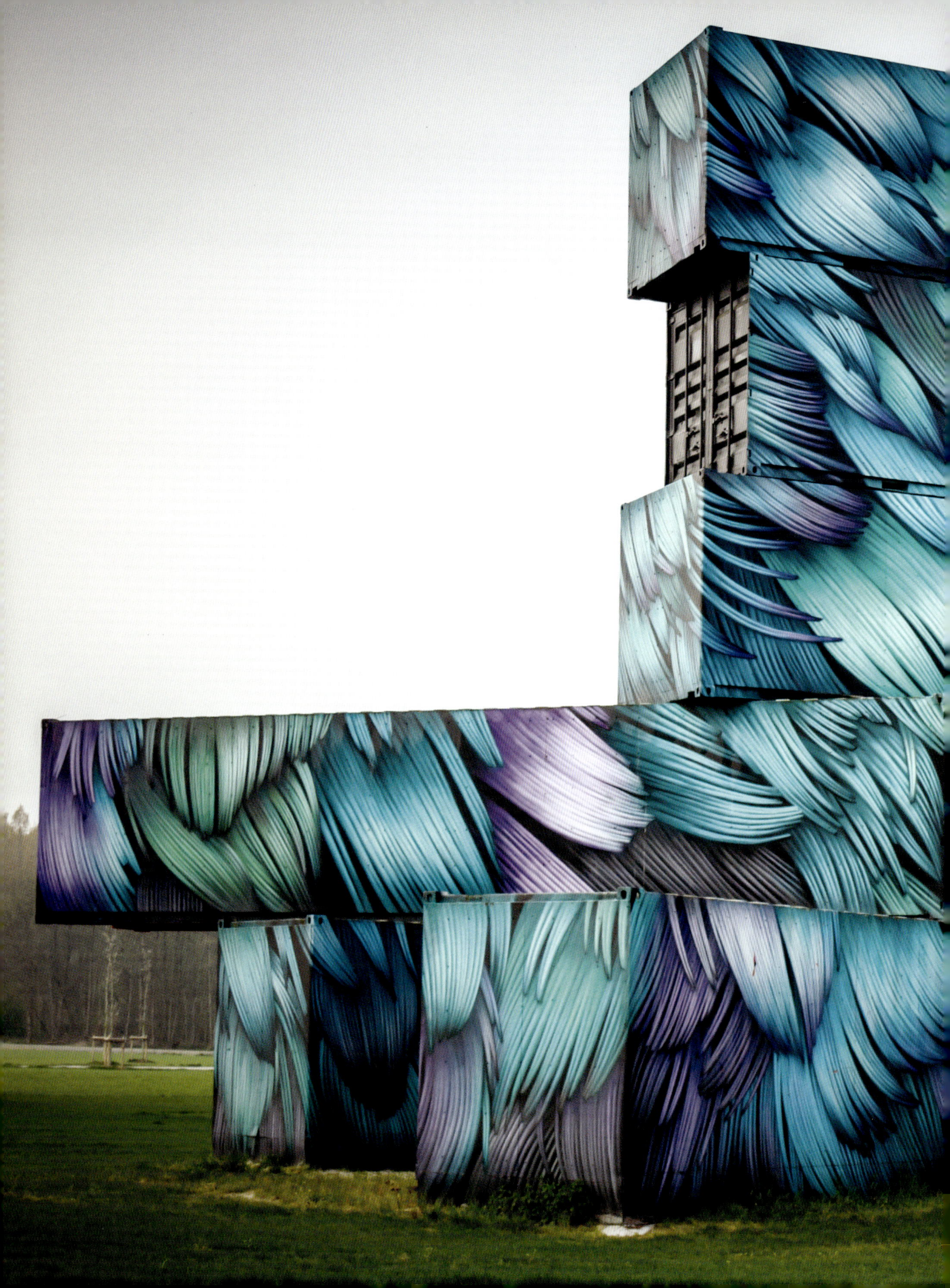

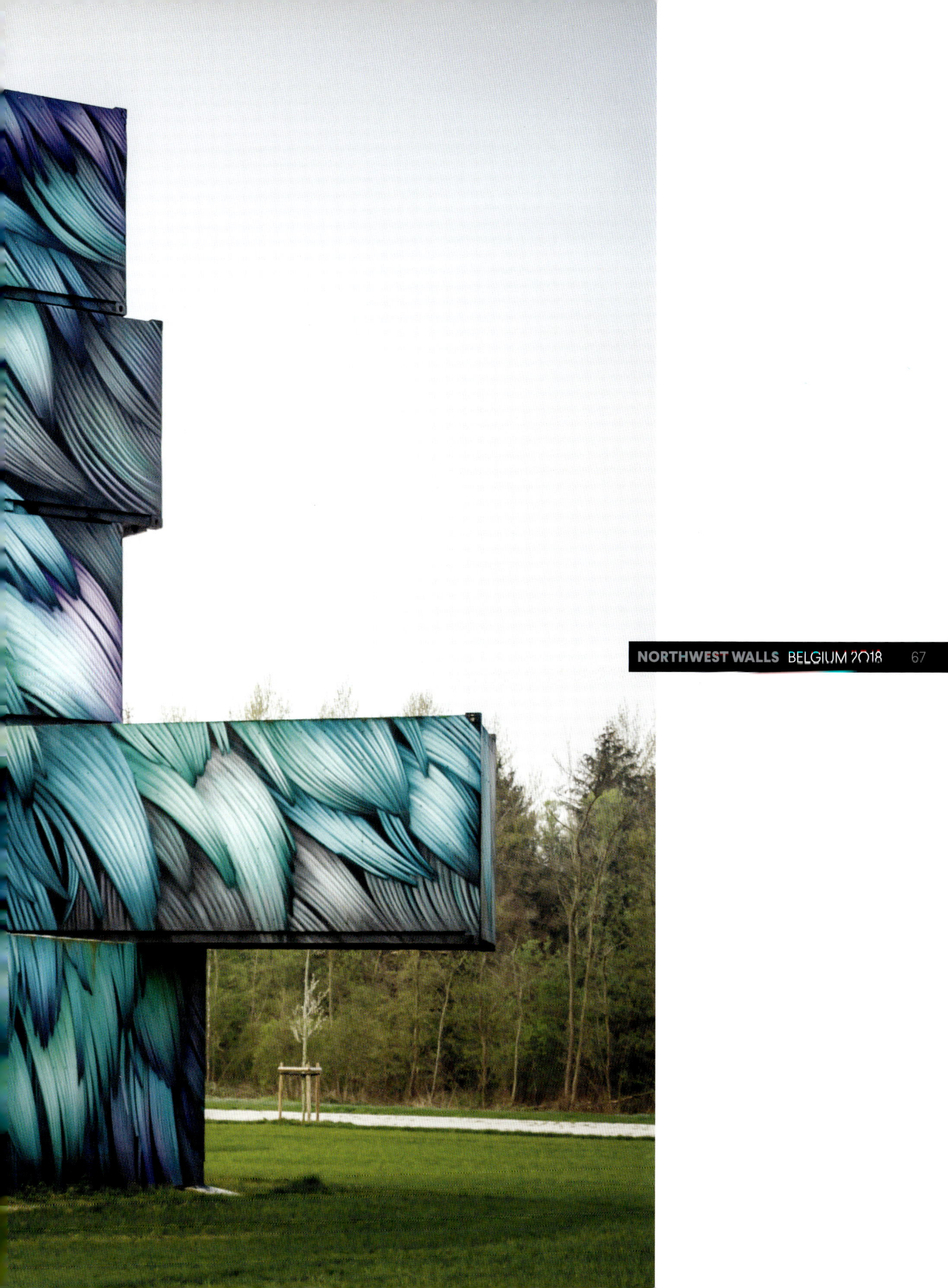

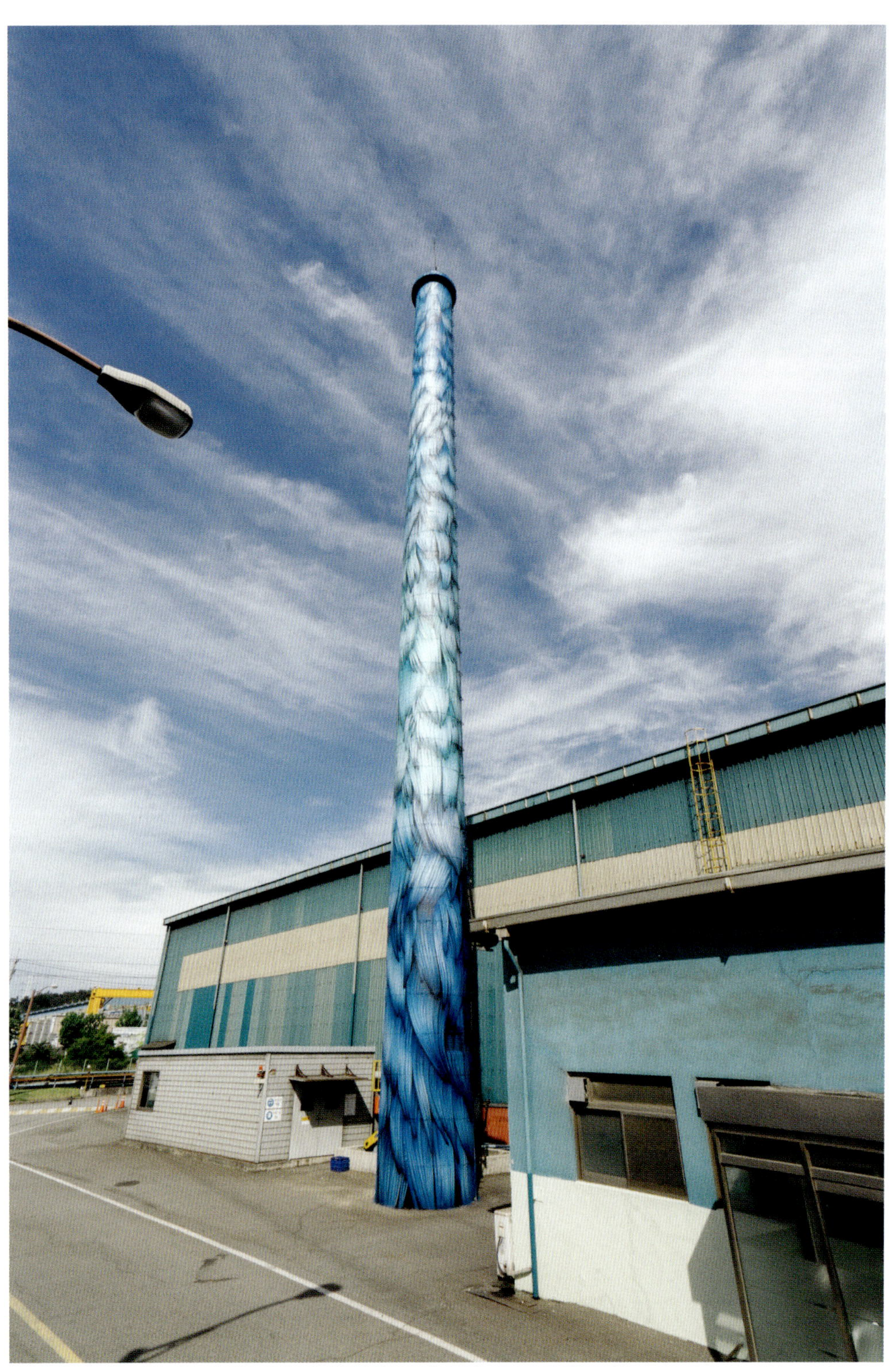

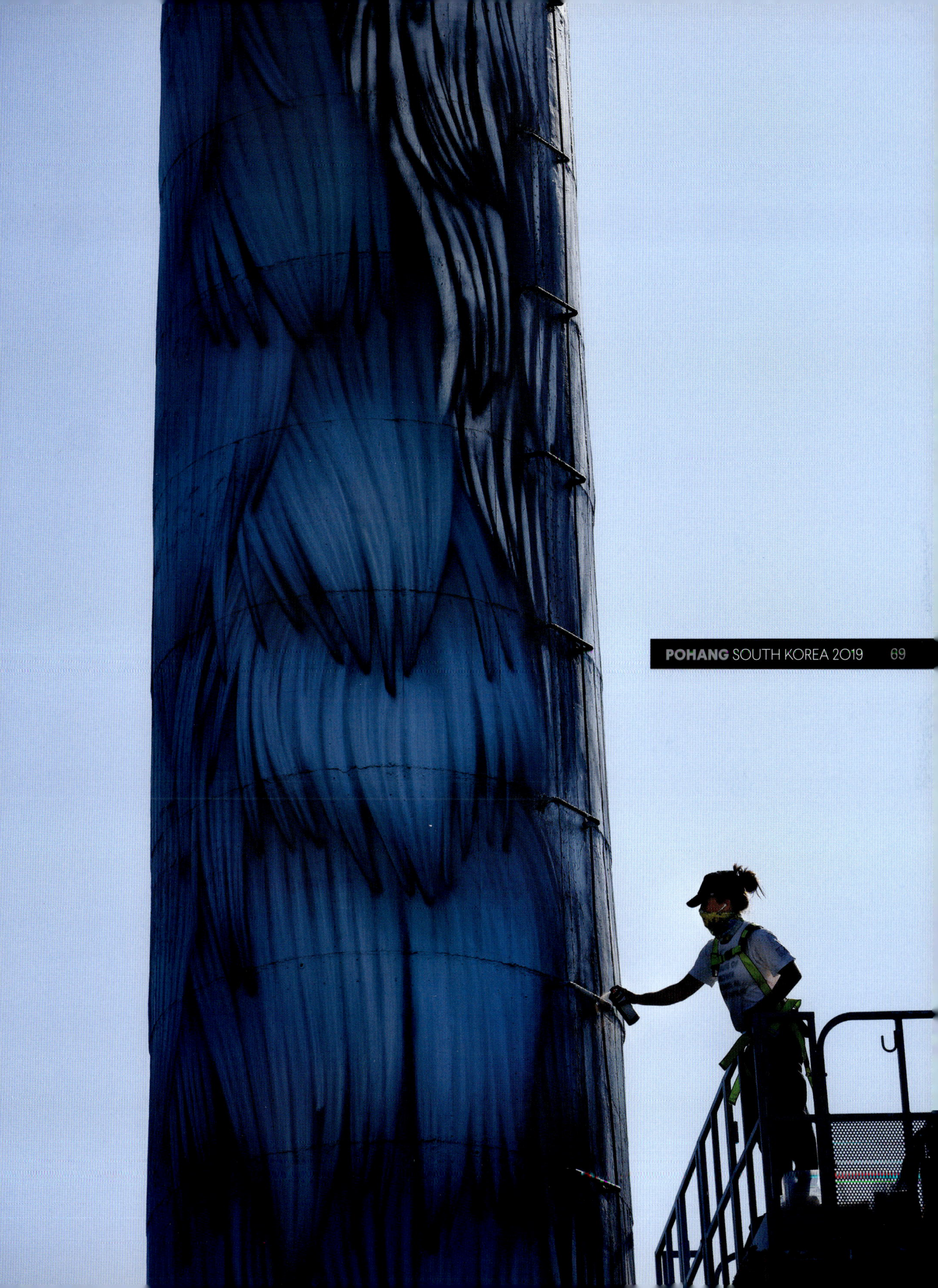
POHANG SOUTH KOREA 2019   69

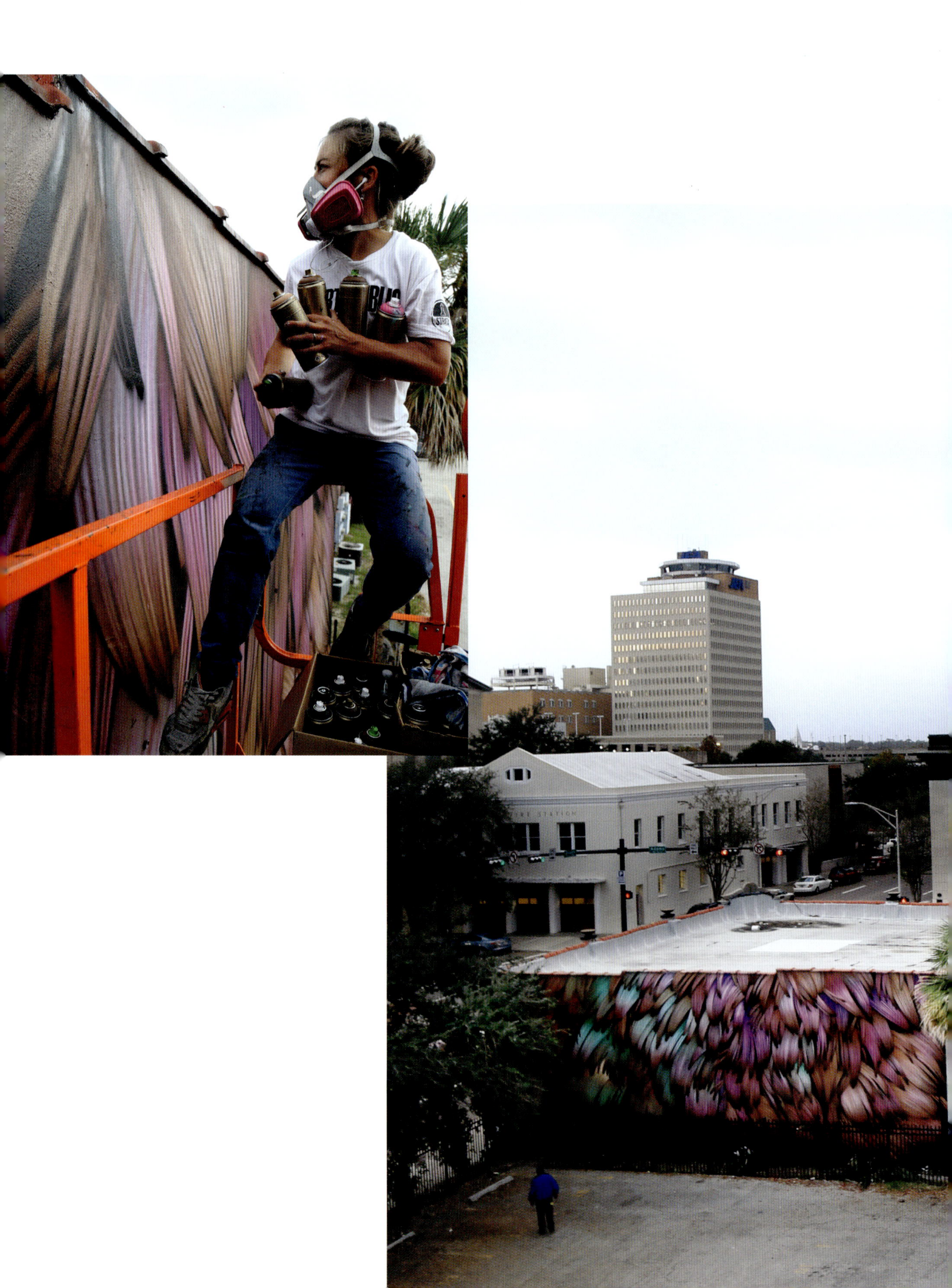

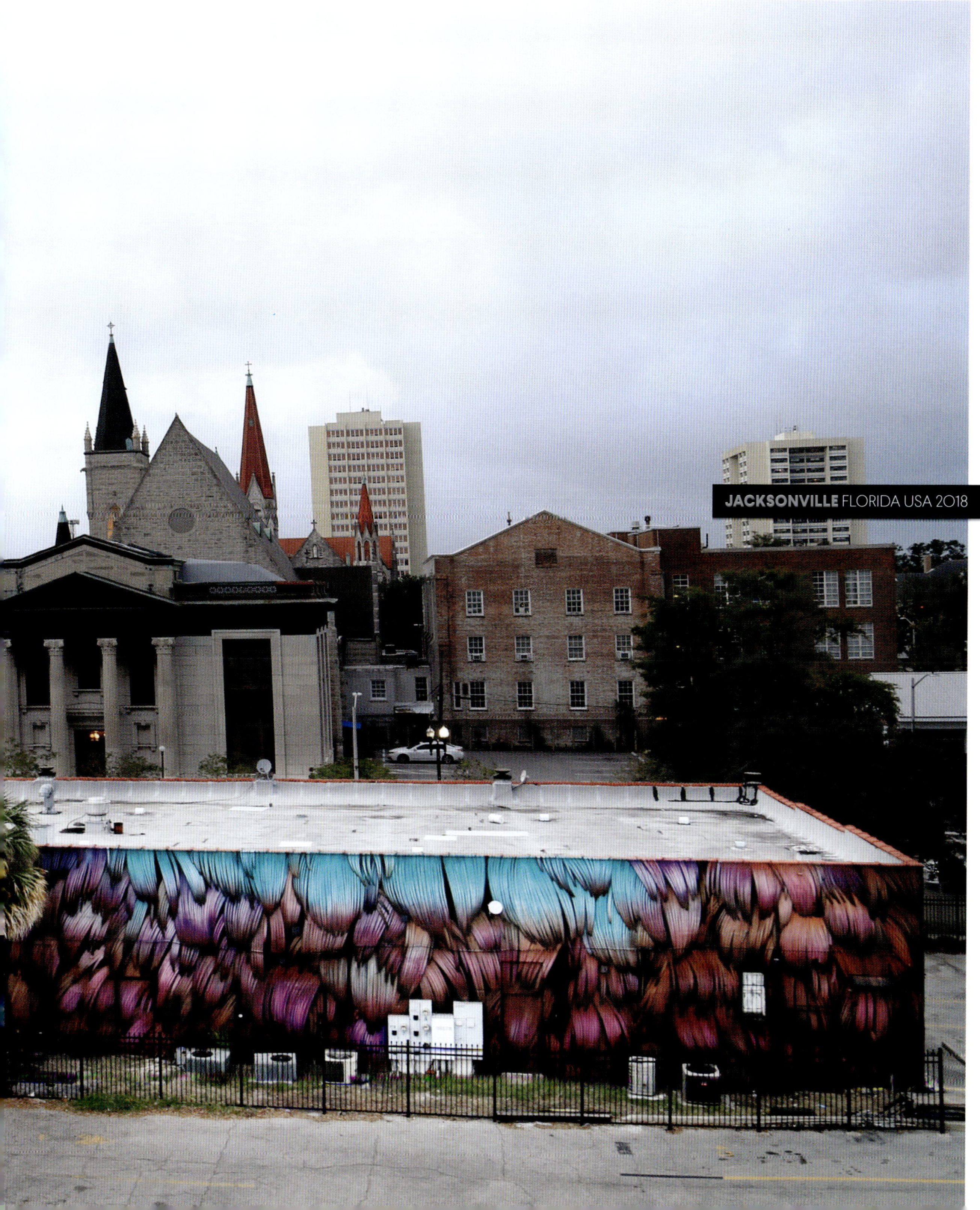

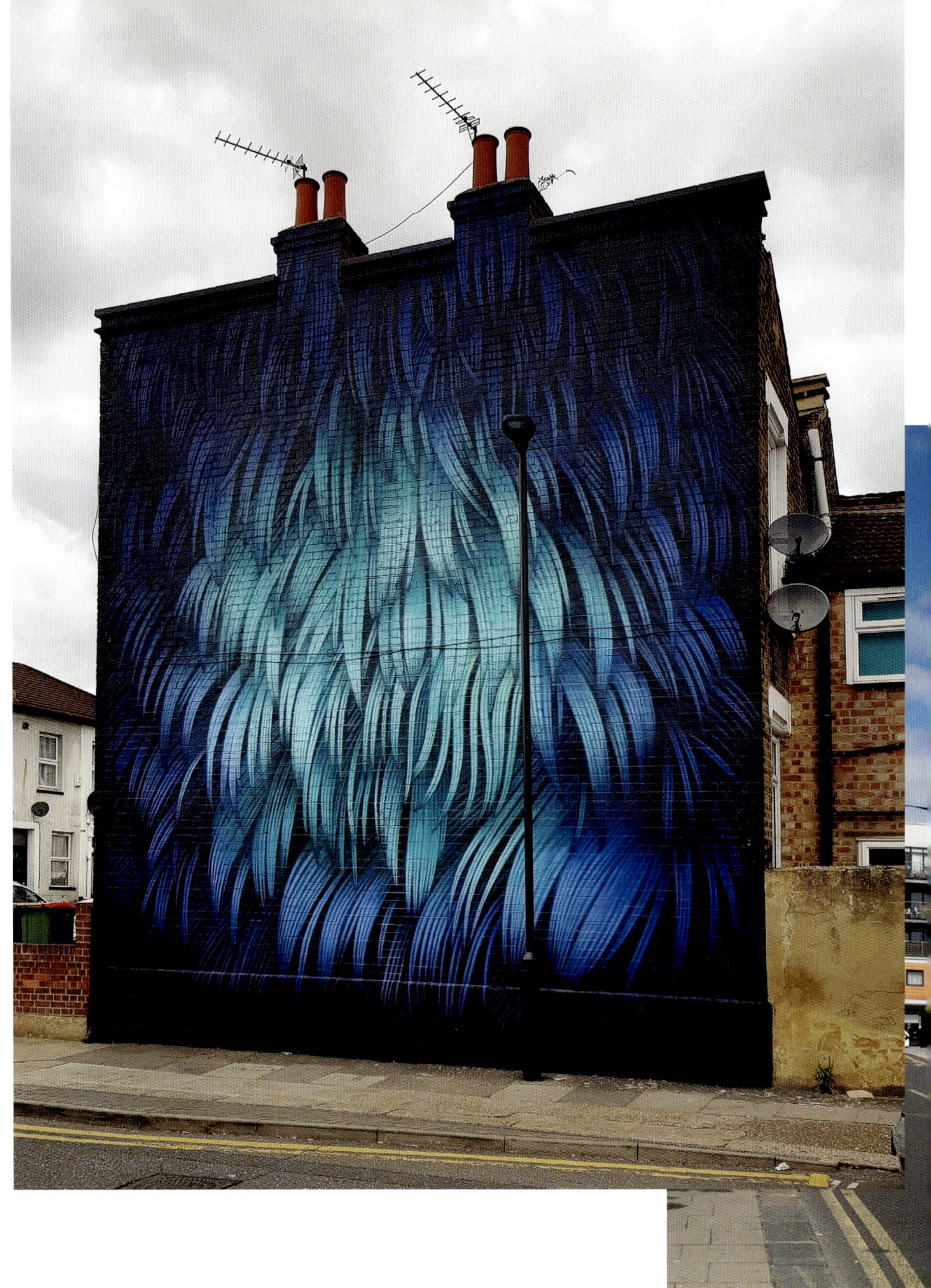

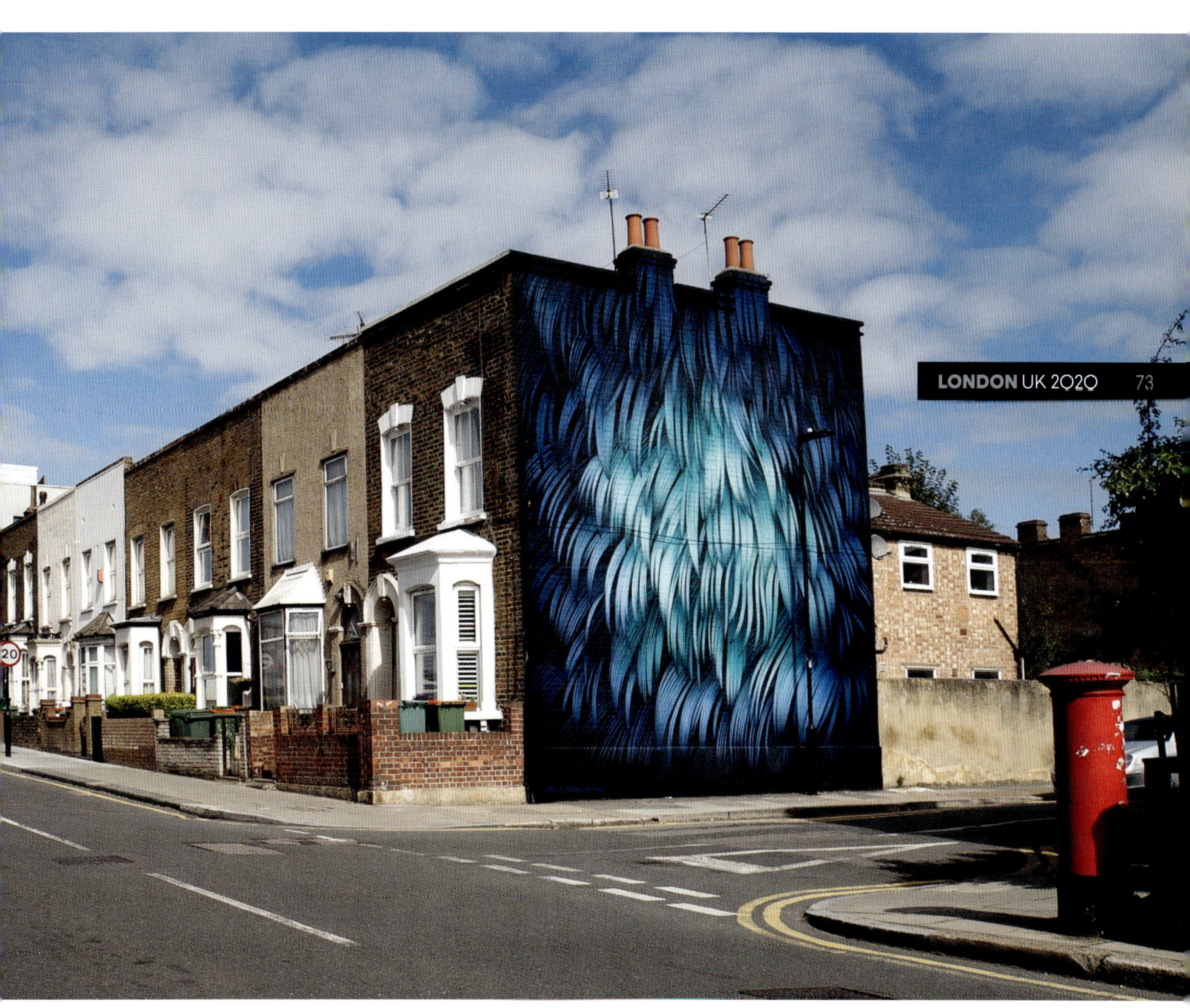

LONDON UK 2020   73

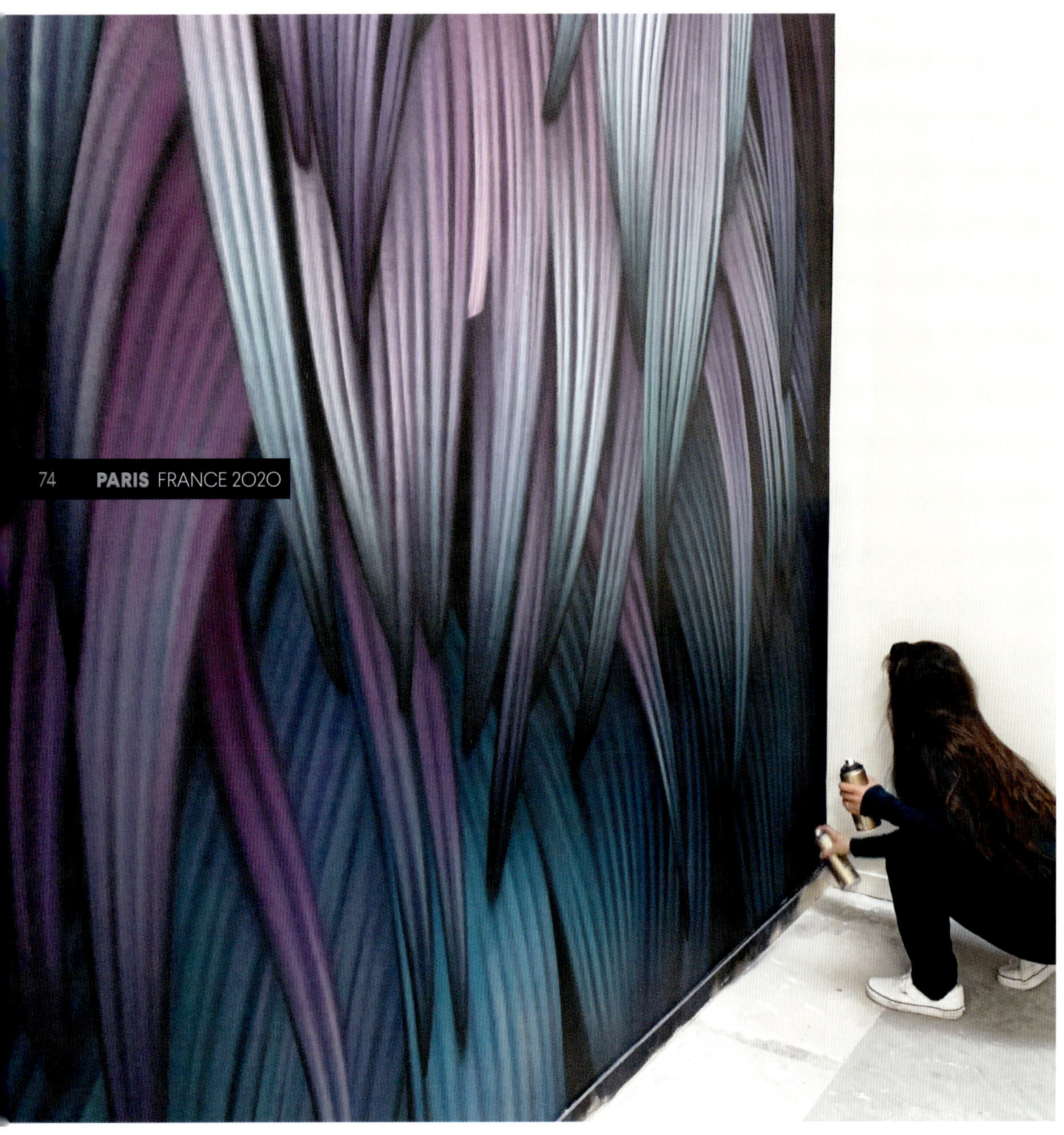
74   PARIS FRANCE 2020

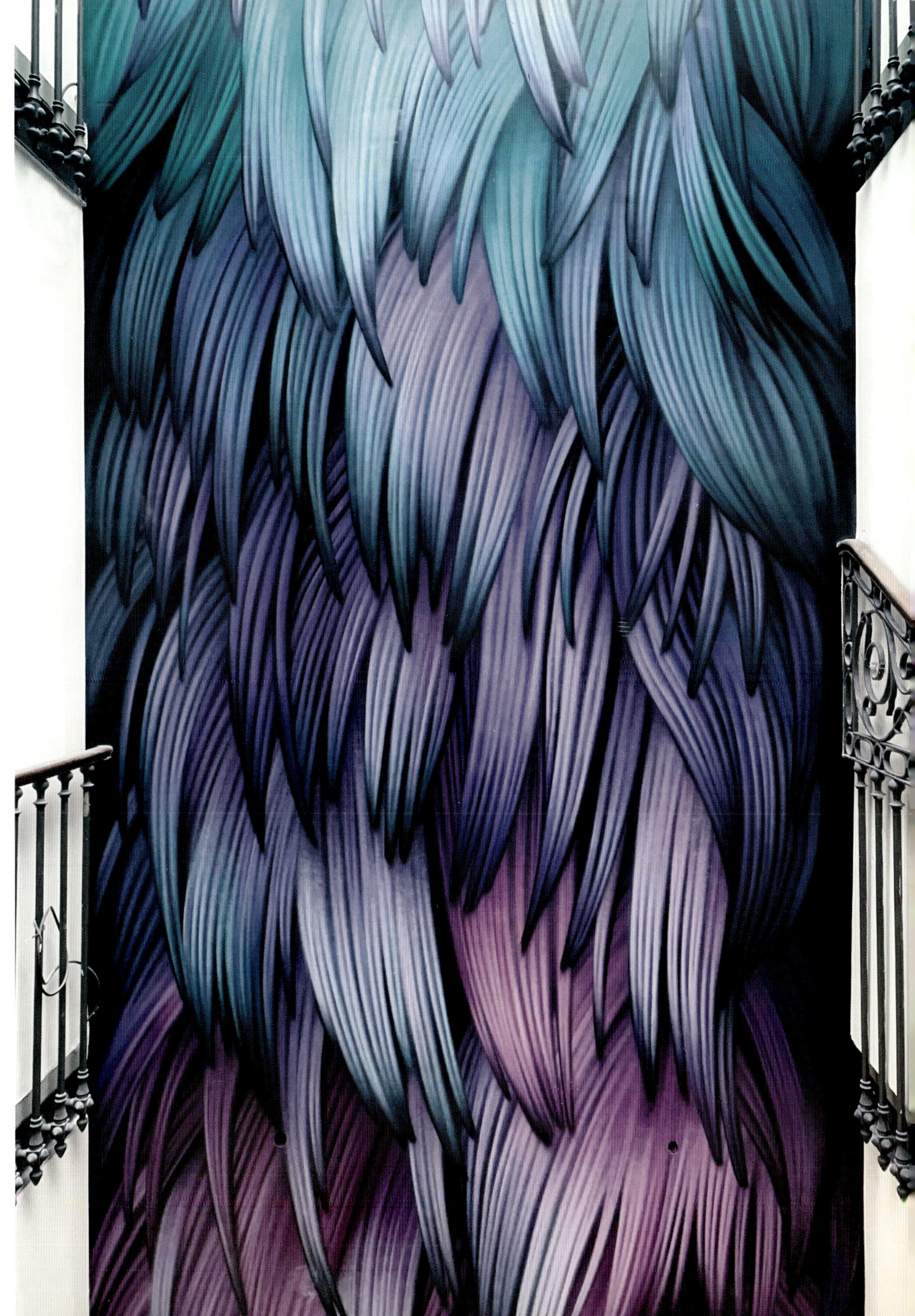

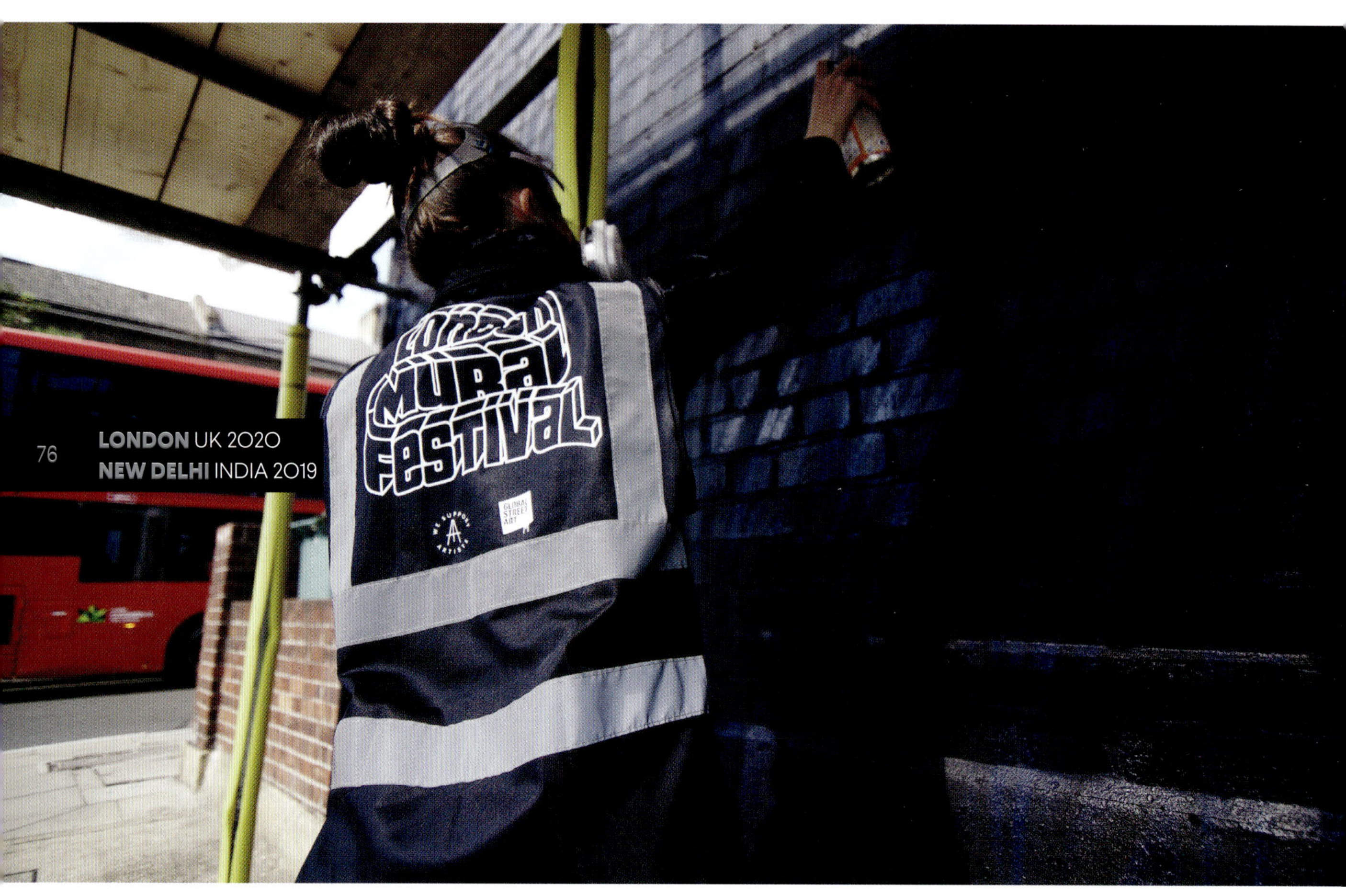

LONDON UK 2020
NEW DELHI INDIA 2019

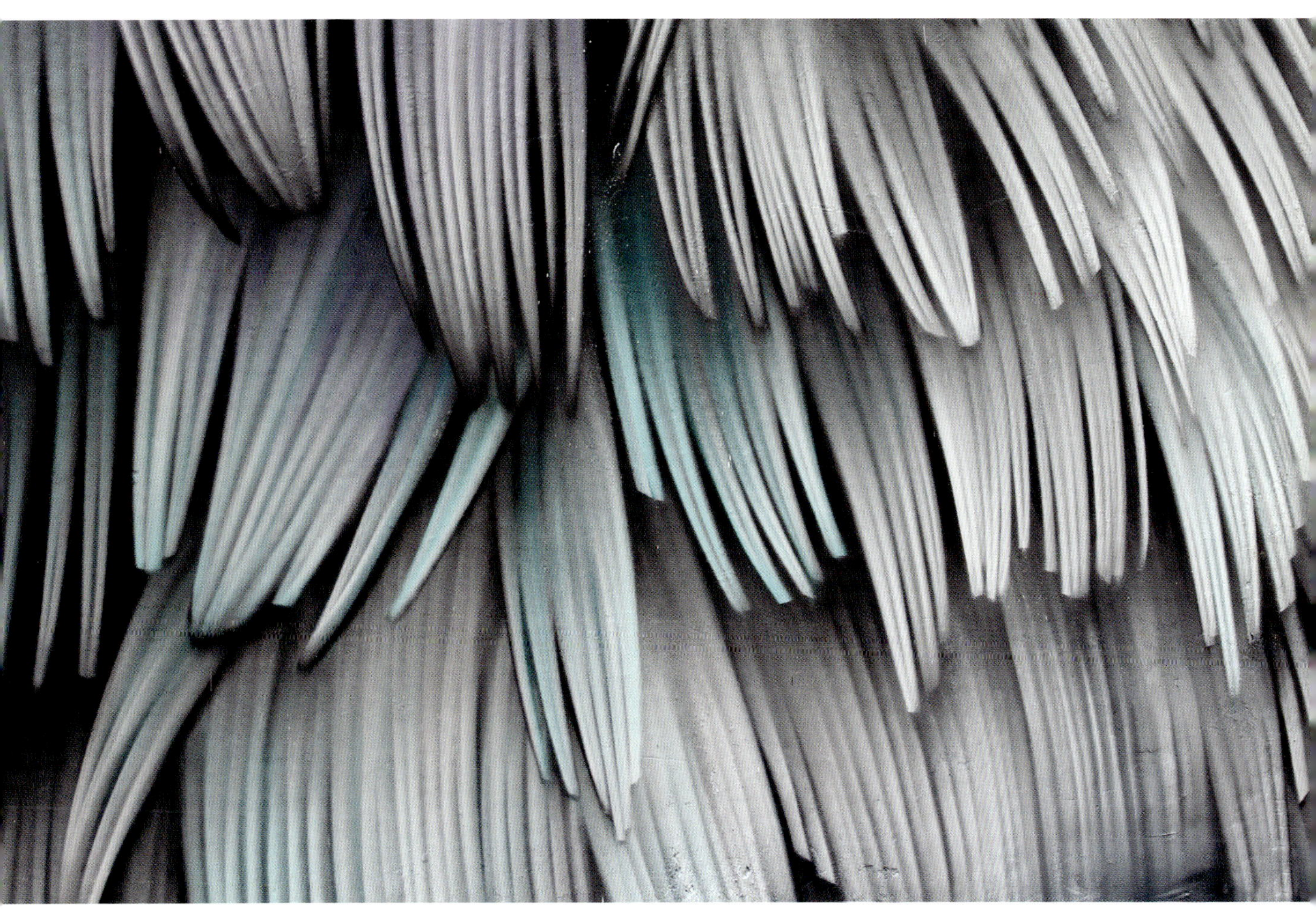

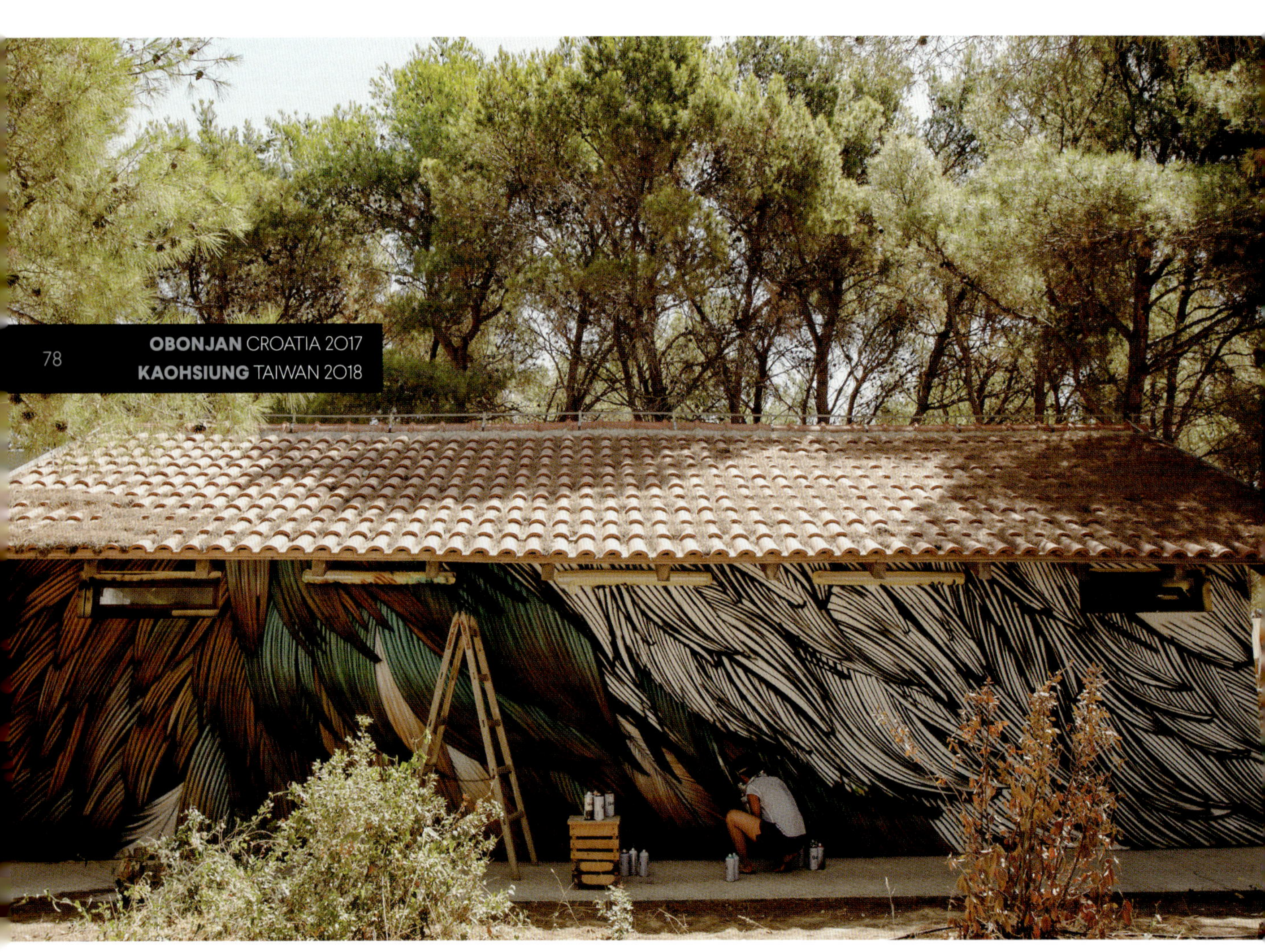
78
OBONJAN CROATIA 2017
KAOHSIUNG TAIWAN 2018

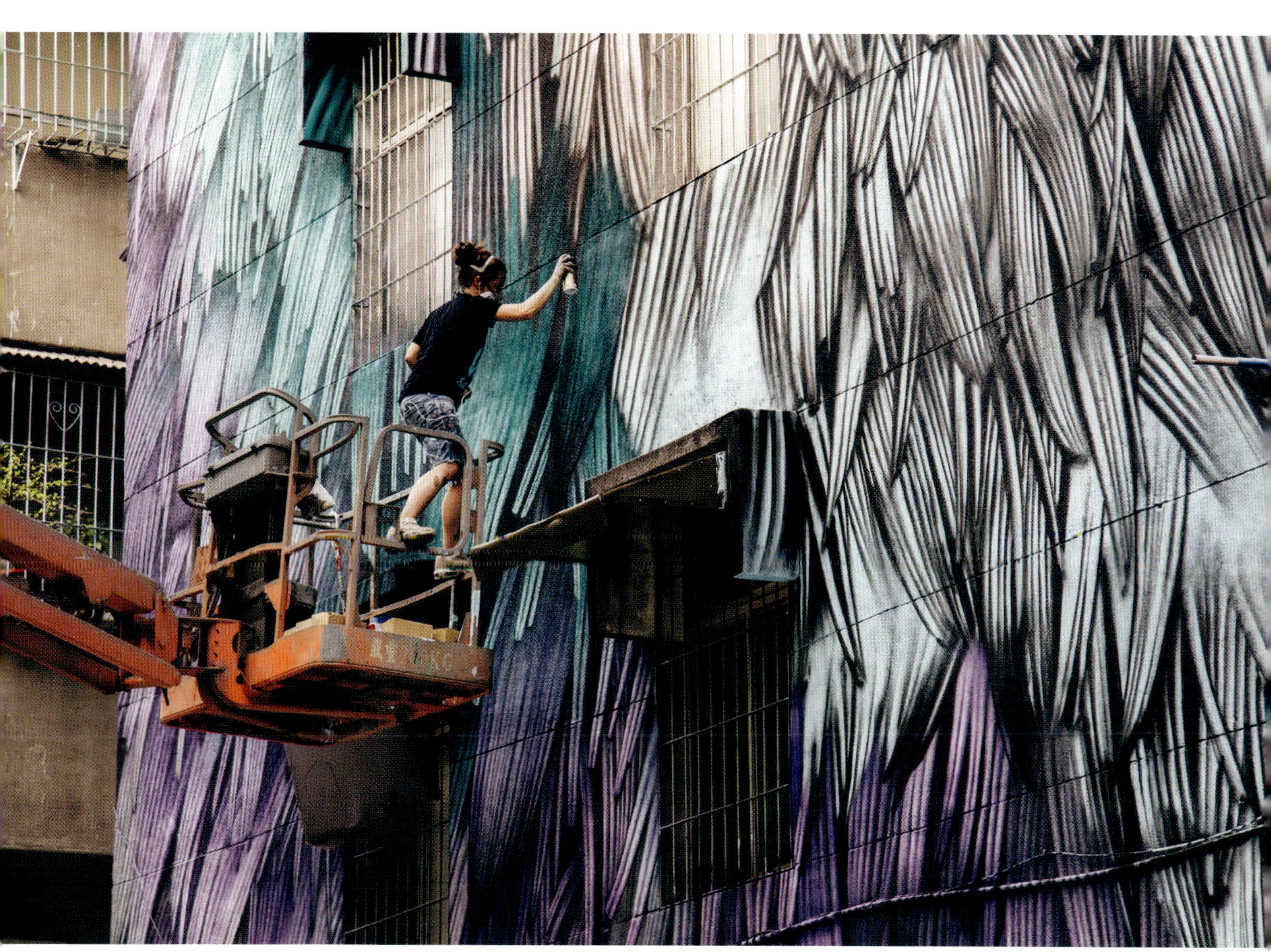

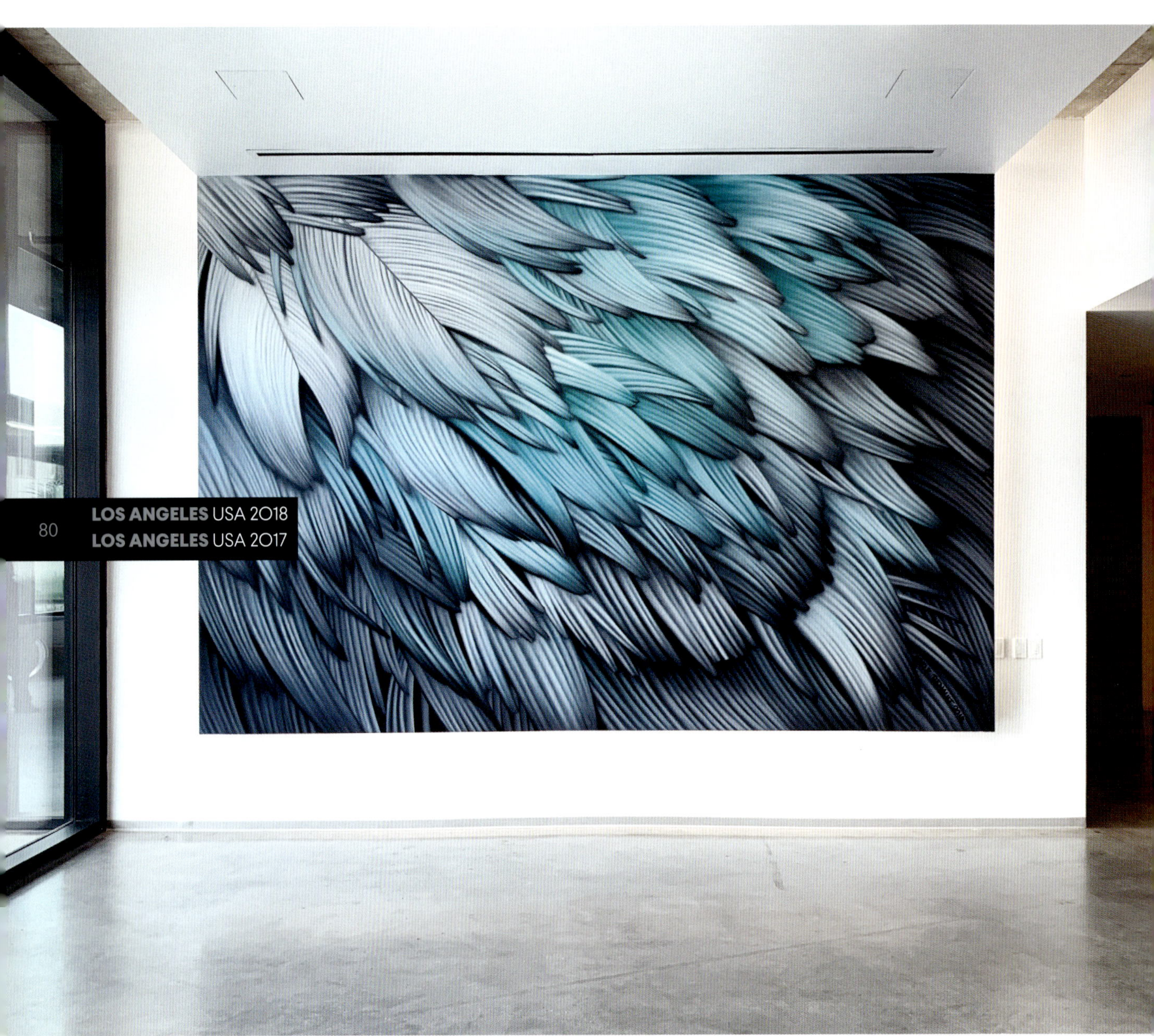
80
LOS ANGELES USA 2018
LOS ANGELES USA 2017

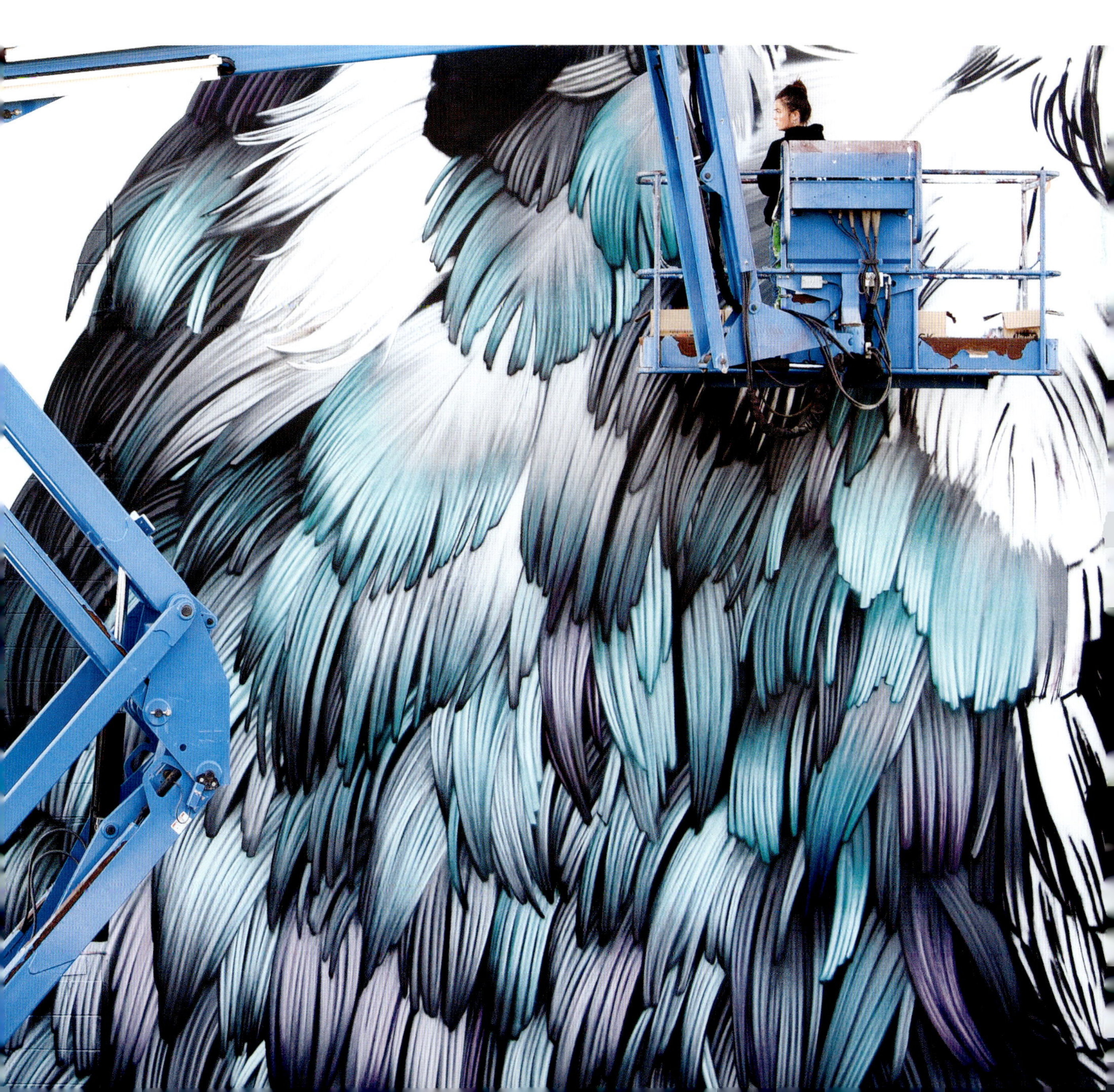

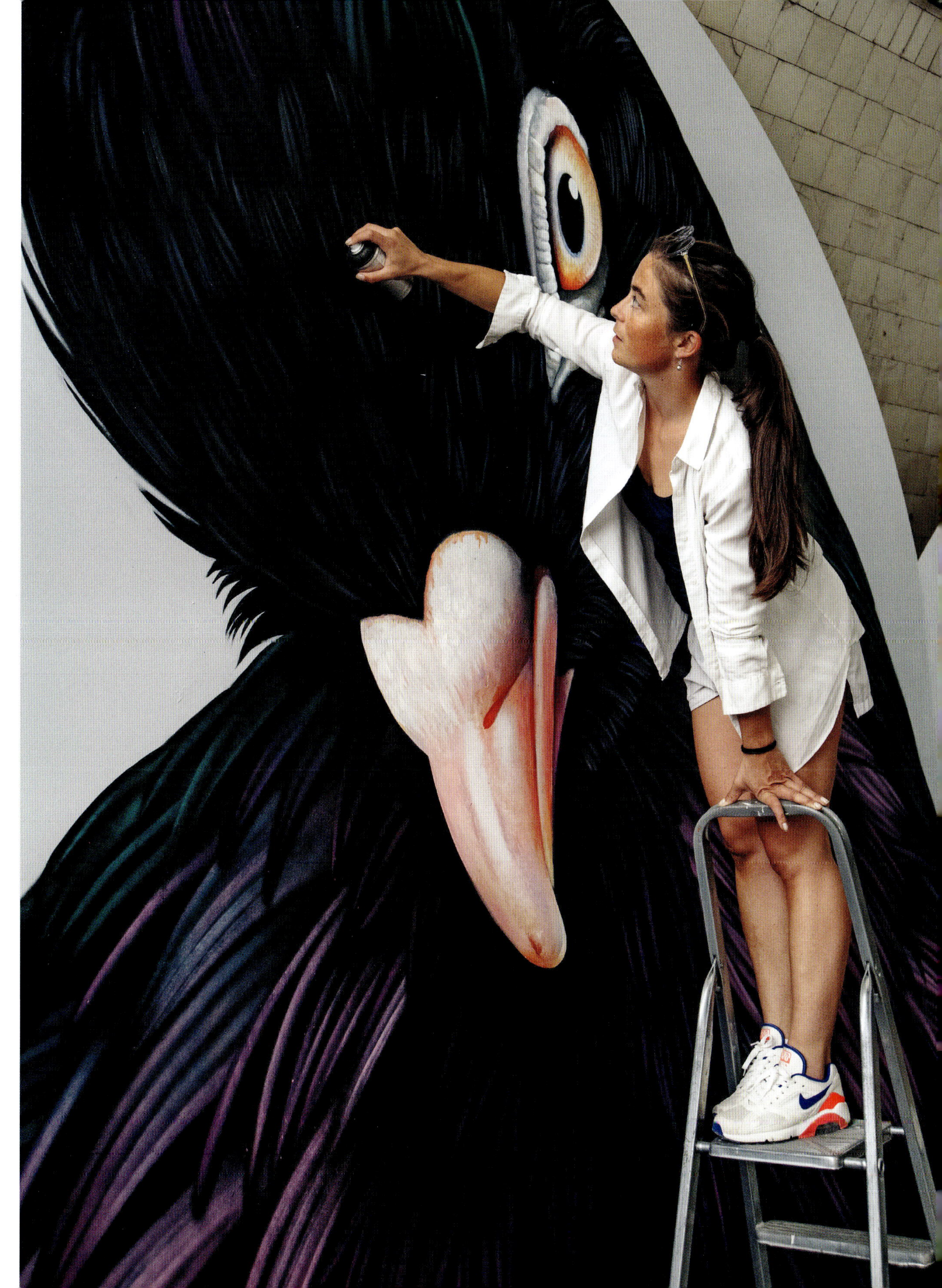

BIOGRAPHY

biographie

Adele Renault is an artist with a deft touch for that which most might find commonplace. From pigeons to people, she focuses her artistry on realistic depictions of ordinary city residents, on canvas as well large scale murals.

Adele was raised on a farm in the Belgian Ardennes where her musical family encouraged her to travel and experience the world on her own. At just fourteen she ventured to Venezuela for a semester and then on to Brighton, England. During her travels she studied visual arts from classical oil painting to modern spray can graffiti, while experimenting with new media and graphic design. Renault graduated in 2010 from the Académie Royale des Beaux Arts in Brussels.

Following her instinct and desire to paint, Adele continues to live her vocation all over the world. Through her solo exhibitions, the United States marks a decisive step in her artistic career. The diversity of humanity and avifauna of American cities becomes the fertile ground for her pictorial aspirations. Her interest in people and pigeons stems from the commonality that no matter the city, each can be found in abundance. It makes her work is immediately relatable. In October 2019, during the exhibition *Crossing Lines* at PDP Gallery, Adele presents a series of portraits of the community that surrounds her studio based in West Adams, Los Angeles.

Through her series, *Gutter Paradise*, started in 2016, Adele has pushed her practice towards a meticulous study of a detail that has become the subject. She forcefully alters an element that might seem banal to make it the main focus of her research.

Adèle Renault est une artiste dotée d'une profonde acuité pour observer ce que la plupart d'entre-nous trouve banal. Des pigeons aux humains, elle concentre son travail artistique sur la représentation des citadins ordinaires sur des toiles ou sur des murs du monde entier.

Adèle a grandi en Ardenne Belge, où sa famille de musiciens l'a encouragée à partir seule à la découverte du monde. A 14 ans à peine, elle s'est rendue au Venezuela et ensuite à Brighton en Angleterre. Durant ses voyages, elle a étudié les arts graphiques, de la peinture aux graffitis modernes, tout en expérimentant aussi les nouveaux media et le design. En 2010, elle a été diplômée de l'Académie Royale des Beaux-Arts de Bruxelles.

Suivant son instinct et son envie de peindre, Adèle continue de vivre sa vocation aux quatre coins du monde. Au gré de ses expositions personnelles, les États-Unis sont pour elle une étape décisive de sa carrière artistique. La diversité de l'humanité et de l'avifaune des métropoles américaines devient le terreau fertile de ses aspirations picturales. Installée dans le quartier de West Adams à Los Angeles, Adèle présente en Octobre 2019, lors de l'exposition *Crossing Lines* à la PDP Gallery, une série de portraits de la communauté qui l'entoure. Avec une technique de portraits si particulière, axée sur l'omniprésence des pigeons et des gens dans nos centres urbains, son travail est aisément reconnaissable.

Au travers de sa série, *Gutter Paradise*, Adèle Renault fait évoluer sa peinture depuis 2016 vers une étude minutieuse d'un détail devenu le sujet. Elle transpose avec conviction un élément qui pourrait sembler anodin pour en faire le centre principal de sa recherche.

EXHIBITIONS

expositions

2020

UN DETAIL DEVENU SUJET
Solo Show
PDP Gallery/Urban Art Fair
Paris, France

SWAY
Group show
Moberg Gallery
Des Moines, IA, USA

2019

CROSSING LINES
Group show
PDP Gallery
Los Angeles, CA, USA

IN BLOOM
Group show
Moberg Gallery
Des Moines, IA, USA

WHERE ART YOU?
Group show
PDP Gallery
Los Angeles, CA, USA

25: IN BLACK & WHITE
Group show
Juxtapoz / Vans / South Beach
Miami, FL, USA

2018

TYSON'S CORNER
Solo show
Ring Side Lounge
NJ, USA

URBAN LEGENDS
Group show
Antler Gallery
Portland, OR. USA

2017

LOLLAPALOOZA
Group show
Urban Nation
Berlin, Germany

ON POINT
Group show
1AM Gallery
San Francisco, CA, USA

FLYING HOME
Solo show
Xi Tang Museum
Beijing, China

2016

LES HOMMES INTÈGRES
Solo show
Art is just a four letter word Gallery
Soest, Germany

SAINT NICHOLAS CATHEDRAL
Group show
Unit44
Newcastle, UK

BRICK TO CANVAS
Tinney Contemporary
Nashville, USA

D'APRÈS NATURE
Group show
Musée des Beaux-Arts de Verviers
Belgium

MACHT
Group show
Gallery Vriend van Bavink
Amsterdam, Netherlands

2015

3D
Trio show
Yoko Uhoda Gallery
Liege, Belgium

#CAMPTHEPIGEON
Solo show
The Annex
Chicago, USA

PIGEON VOYAGEUR
Solo show
Art is just a four letter word gallery
Soest, Germany

2014

LES CLOCHARDS CÉLESTES
Solo show
White Walls
San Francisco, USA

2013

PIGEON PORTRAITS
With Lisa Roze
Unruly Gallery
Amsterdam, Netherlands

REPEAT CLUB
Group show
Witzenhausen Gallery
Amsterdam, Netherlands

2012

WE THE ARTISTS
Group Show
Unruly Gallery
Amsterdam, Netherlands

BLACK LIVES MATTER